KINGS, COMMONERS, and COLONISTS

Puritan Politics in Old New England, 1603–1660

Selma R.Williams

Atheneum
1975 *New York*

To Burt

48060

Copyright © 1974 by Selma R. Williams
All rights reserved
Library of Congress catalog card number 73-84840
ISBN 0-689-30150-2
Published simultaneously in Canada by
McClelland & Stewart, Ltd.
Manufactured in the United States of America by
Halliday Lithograph Corporation
West Hanover, Massachusetts
Designed by Harriett Barton
First Printing January 1974
Second Printing October 1975

Introduction

"Massachusetts: The One and Only"

The Presidential election of 1972 produced motto-mania in Massachusetts: "State of Awareness"; "The Lone Star State"; "Massachusetts—We'd Rather Be Right." Fifty-five percent of Massachusetts voters publicly congratulated themselves for having exhibited extreme individualism. They had given Democratic challenger George S. McGovern his single state victory, contrasted with the forty-nine states that supported incumbent President Richard M. Nixon.

These Massachusetts moderns were throwbacks to the state's ancient individualistic past, 1630–1660, when the Bay Colony began its unique existence. In fact, another 1972 slogan would have summed up the situation way back then: "Massachusetts—The One and Only." Never before in history had colonists elected their own officials, instituted representative government, designed and flown their own flag after refusing to hoist the motherland's colors, pursued their own foreign policy, tried their own civil and criminal offenders, published their own code of laws, or coined their own money.

In addition, there was the beginning of the Eastern Establishment. Harvard College was set up in 1636. Cambridge was the site of the first printing press in English America in 1638. And in 1647, the Massachusetts legislature passed a law requiring every town to supply funds to support its own public school.

The events in old England that allowed New England men and women to get away with a full generation of political independence and innovation form the story and theme of *Kings, Commoners, and Colonists*. The book formally begins in 1603, with the first *"King"* of the title, James I. But two sixteenth-century predecessors, Henry VIII and Elizabeth, demand at least a brief prologue appearance. Even after death, these Tudor monarchs continued to exert tremendous influence on the interplay of politics in old and New England.

Contents

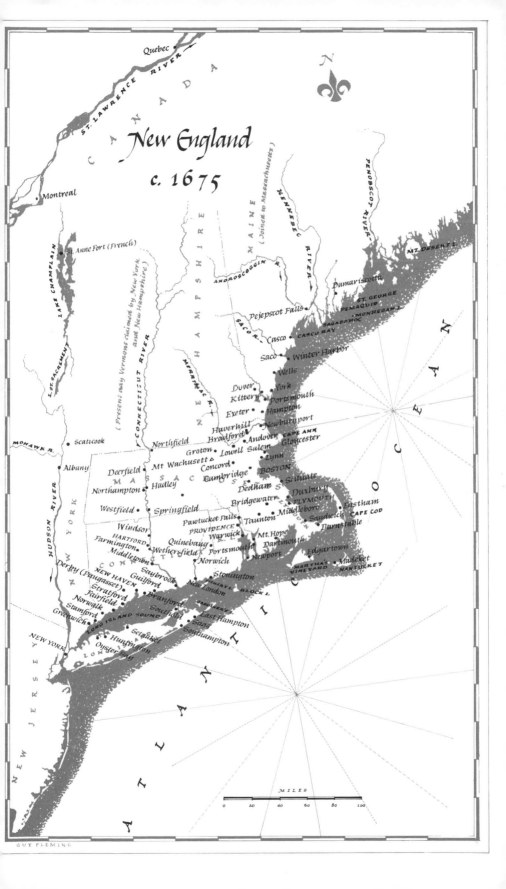

New England
c. 1675

Quebec

CANADA

ST. LAWRENCE RIVER

Montreal

LAKE CHAMPLAIN

St. Anne Fort (French)

L. St. SACREMENT

MOHAWK R.

Scaticook

Albany

HUDSON RIVER

NEW YORK

NEW JERSEY

NEW YORK

N

(Present day Vermont claimed by New York and New Hampshire)

CONNECTICUT RIVER

NEW HAMPSHIRE

MERRIMACK R.

MAINE
(Joined to Massachusetts)

KENNEBEC RIVER

PENOBSCOT RIVER

MT. DESERT I.

ANDROSCOGGIN R.

SACO R.

Damariscotta

ST. GEORGE

PEMAQUID

SAGADAHOC

MONHEGAN I.

Pejepscot Falls

Casco

CASCO BAY

Saco

Winter Harbor

Wells

Dover

Kittery

York

Portsmouth

Exeter

Hampton

Haverhill

Bradford

Newburyport

Northfield

Groton

Andover

CAPE ANN

Mt Wachusett

Lowell

Salem

Gloucester

Concord

Lynn

Deerfield

MASSACHUSETTS

Cambridge

BOSTON

Northampton

Hadley

Dedham

Scituate

Westfield

Springfield

Bridgewater

Duxbury

PLYMOUTH

Pawtucket Falls

Taunton

Middleboro

Eastham

Windsor

PROVIDENCE

Sandwich

CAPE COD

Farmington

HARTFORD

Quinebaug

Warwick

Mt. Hope

Barnstable

Middletown

Wethersfield

Portsmouth

Dartmouth

Derby (Paugasset)

CONNECTICUT

Norwich

Newport

Edgartown

NEW HAVEN

Saybrook

Stonington

MARTHA'S VINEYARD

Nantucket

Stratford

Guilford

New London

NANTUCKET

Fairfield

Branford

RHODE ISLAND

BLOCK I.

Norwalk

Southold

Stamford

East Hampton

Greenwich

LONG ISLAND SOUND

Setauket

Sag

Southampton

Huntington

Oyster Bay

ATLANTIC OCEAN

MILES

0   20   40   60   80   100

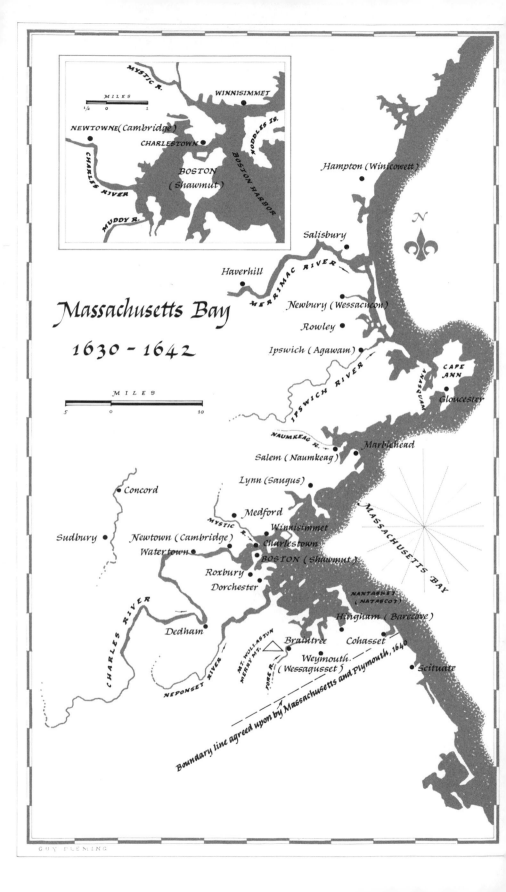

Massachusetts Bay

1630 – 1642

Inset map:

WINNISIMMET

MYSTIC R.

NEWTOWNE (Cambridge)

CHARLESTOWN

NODDLES IS.

BOSTON (Shawmut)

BOSTON HARBOR

CHARLES RIVER

MUDDY R.

MILES
1/2 0 1

Main map:

Hampton (Winicowett)

Salisbury

Haverhill

MERRIMAC RIVER

Newbury (Wessacucon)

Rowley

Ipswich (Agawam)

IPSWICH RIVER

CAPE ANN

Gloucester

ANNISQUAM

NAUMKEAG R.

Marblehead

Salem (Naumkeag)

Lynn (Saugus)

Concord

Medford

MYSTIC R.

Winnisimmet

Sudbury

Newtown (Cambridge)

Charlestown

Watertown

BOSTON (Shawmut)

Roxbury

Dorchester

MASSACHUSETTS BAY

CHARLES RIVER

Dedham

NANTASKET (NATASCOT)

Hingham (Barecove)

Braintree

Cohasset

MT. WOLLASTON
MERRY MT.

Weymouth (Wessagusset)

FORE R.

Scituate

NEPONSET RIVER

Boundary line agreed upon by Massachusetts and Plymouth, 1640

MILES
5 0 10

N

GUY FLEMING

Prologue

Everything Queen Elizabeth touched turned to power for England. "Gloriana" an affectionate nation called her.

She was the last and best loved of the fabled dynasty of Tudors. Like her grandfather Henry VII and her father Henry VIII, her private life brightened society with gossip, sometimes obscuring the greater glories of her public life.

In an age that despised women, she was Europe's strongest, most effective monarch. Coyly she told her subjects, "I know I have the body of a weak and feeble woman," then added fiercely, "but I have the heart and stomach of a king, and of a king of England too." She laid indestructible foundations at home for a prosperous and unified England, and for a strong middle class. Abroad she bested her enemies, France and Spain, clearing the seas all the way to the New World.

In effect Elizabeth reversed the old adage to read, "Behind every great woman there is a man." In the case of Good Queen Bess, there were two men. Her grandfather Henry VII had founded the Tudor dynasty in 1485 by defeating the

3

last of the feudal barons who had made separate and conflicting claims to rule wide sections of England. Her father, Henry VIII, nationalized the Church and dissolved the Catholic monasteries, thereby making the Pope powerless in English affairs. Whether by brilliant scheming or lucky accident, two major advantages followed. The King profited from sale of the monastic lands, thus bypassing the need for additional taxes. And at the same time he established a new land-owning class to counterbalance the ever-present, though defeated, barons.

Until the victory of the Tudors in 1485, life in England had been a procession of crises, anarchy, and unspeakable conditions for hundreds of years. The Middle Ages had produced the great English language, the Magna Carta with its foundations for trial by jury, and the glimmerings of Parliamentary government. Yet Englishmen continued to suffer from starvation, plague, and constant baronial wars for land control.

Only England's island isolation protected her people from another menace, land invasion during Europe's bloodletting wars. Following the Norman conquest of 1066, she had been untouched by hostile foreigners. Intent on keeping her distance, England even refused to follow largely Catholic Europe in adopting the Gregorian calendar in 1582. As the inspiration of the Roman Catholic Pope Gregory XIII, the common sense of catching up with the true vernal equinox by canceling ten days would never do for Protestant England. So for almost two centuries—until 1752—England lived in happy pagan confusion, observing the 45 B.C. calendar of Julius Caesar, ten days behind Europe. And the English new year began not on January 1, but in seeding time, the month of March.

However, England's isolation proved a mixed blessing when it delayed for about a century the arrival in England of the Renaissance, that miracle of emphasis on human dignity.

In the rain-sodden, virtually sunless land of Elizabeth, the Renaissance came to dwell on the art of government, rather than on painting and sculpture. England nurtured constitutionalism, the basis of modern representative government, while Italy—blazing forth with sun, color, and foreign contacts—produced Botticelli, Leonardo da Vinci, and Michelangelo.

The largely unwritten English Constitution, defining the role and prestige of Parliament and concern for the individual, grew significantly under Elizabeth. To unify the country against a resurgence of powerful feudal lords, the Queen had had to strengthen the monarchy. In turn, an effective monarchy needed the support of Parliament, which represented all areas of the kingdom.

Again the Tudor timing was either devastatingly shrewd or fatefully lucky. The newly strengthened—and often university-trained—middle class of merchants, landowners, and professional men began actively seeking representation or service in the House of Commons. Previously such service had been considered a meaningless and loathsome chore. Now under Elizabeth's skillful handling, Commons membership gave the appearance of a certain amount of authority—plus immediate entry into high society.

The House of Lords, where the nobility sat, was rapidly losing its superior position in Parliament to the House of Commons dominated by the new middle class. Increasingly, Elizabeth allowed Commons to assert rights to make laws and vote taxes—with royal assent of course—and, under certain conditions, to discuss grievances. The Queen's firm refusal to entertain the idea of interference with her sovereign power in making foreign policy and in solving religious problems aroused little argument. These fields had not as yet assumed the overriding importance of levying taxes and formulating laws.

During her forty-five year reign Elizabeth had made few visible mistakes as she established stability at home and won naval supremacy abroad. Even her possibly dangerous delay in naming a successor attracted praise. Political wise men claimed to sense some deeply secret but definitely shrewd political motive. Actually, the reason hovered somewhere between procrastination and fear of assassination by a rival group eager to put its own man on the throne.

The execution of her troublesome and Catholic rival, Mary Queen of Scots, and the English defeat of the avenging Spanish Armada one year later brought undisputed authority and dazzling glory to Elizabeth. There were no more challenges to her sovereignty or serious plots against her life. Her occasional lapses into arbitrary rule after 1590 were excused on grounds of senility. The young Elizabeth's accomplishments might be immortal, but the aging and crotchety Elizabeth appeared to be quite mortal. In the nature of things, there would soon have to be a new monarch.

With her usual combination of logic and calculation, Elizabeth secretly decided on a successor. He would be none other than her first cousin twice removed, King James Stuart of Scotland, Protestant son of her mortal enemy Catholic Mary Queen of Scots, and great-grandson of Henry VIII's sister Margaret: England was still hovering between Catholicism and Protestantism. The Protestant son of the Scottish Catholic queen should satisfy both factions. And as a magnificent bonus, James would bring with him the Crown of Scotland, thus ending the threat of a combined French and Scottish invasion from the north. He would be the first King of Great Britain, uniting the Crowns of North Britain (Scotland) and South Britain (England).

As death approached, Elizabeth never spoke the name of James, but began to talk in riddles about her successor: "My seat has been the seat of kings. And I will have no rascal to succeed. Who shall succeed me but a king?"

Moments before two o'clock on Thursday morning, March 24, 1603, those around her deathbed were quite prepared to hear and translate her last faint murmurings into a strong statement concerning her successor: "Who should that be but our cousin of Scotland?"

When the era of the "Faerie Queene" ended in 1603 with the passing of Elizabeth, the gloom and stagnation of the Middle Ages threatened to return, the omen being the recurrence of the dreaded plague of the Middle Ages, which was killing one person out of five in London alone.

Pessimists pointed to another bad omen. The man who would soon be crowned King James I of Great Britain was a foreigner, forbidden under ancient English law to inherit land in England, let alone the kingship.

"Our Cousin of Scotland"

To the joy and relief of Englishmen, the transition from goddesslike Elizabeth to "our cousin of Scotland" occurred peacefully.

"God's wounds. I will pull down my breeches and they shall also see my arse," exulted the new King. For a whole month crowds had been applauding and cheering him everywhere along the 400-mile route from Edinburgh to London. King James VI of feeble Scotland was now King James I of all-powerful Great Britain.

But the uneventful changeover from properly English Elizabeth Tudor to earthily Scottish James Stuart proved deceptive. By the end of his reign James as King had unsettled the Old World as he had provoked settlement of the New. He rocked two continents, setting the stage for the Civil War and Glorious Revolution in England, and for the establishment of fiercely self-sufficient Massachusetts and independence in America.

In the beginning, however, the change of dynasties produced nothing more than a brief skyrocketing in the price of grain, due to hoarding. And even that returned to normal after two days, when no rebellion followed and no signs or hints of trouble appeared.

"God for his house a Steward hath provided," quipped Sir John Harrington, pioneer in the art of epigram. And a minor poet sang:

> Then frolic England, sport in lawful games,
> Make room to entertain matchless King James.

Even plain James waxed poetic, recalling those first meetings with his new subjects, "their eyes flaming nothing but sparkles of affection, their mouths and tongues uttering nothing but sounds of joy, their hands, feet, and all the rest of their members in their gestures discovering a passionate longing and earnestness to meet and embrace their new sovereign."

Indeed, James's future looked dazzling compared to his past as he left Edinburgh early Tuesday morning, April 5, 1603—though he had to admit that he dreaded the long journey on horseback over vast stretches of land filled with rocks and highway robbers. Awkward in all his movements, he was forever falling off horses, sometimes injuring himself severely. However, he could console himself that a few minor accidents might mean just enough delay to insure his arrival in London after Elizabeth's burial. He hated funerals.

Death and misery had filled his youth. Plunging into kingship at the age of eleven months, with no time for childhood, he replaced his mother Mary Queen of Scots in 1567. The nobility had forced the Queen from her throne, preferring to deal with her baby son. As Scotland's child-king, James suffered constant indignities. His mother abandoned him forever when he was one year old. And several times Scottish chieftains toppled him from his throne, kidnapping him at will, returning him when convenient. Death by violence struck his father, Lord Darnley, when James was still less than a year old, and his mother, Queen Mary, when he reached the age of twenty-one. Too young to object to the murder of his father, or to the scandalous hints that his mother was a member of the conspiracy, he was too anxious to win Elizabeth's favor to protest loudly the Queen's order to behead his mother.

Maturity and a certain amount of confidence brought an overriding desire to make himself respectable in the eyes of his countrymen and the world. By the age of twenty-seven he had served as king of Scotland for more than a quarter of a century, and had succeeded in subduing the nobles, thereby unifying the country. So, seven years after the execution of Queen Mary, though he never really knew or loved his parents, he extracted from the Scottish Parliament an act defining slander of his mother or father as treason, punishable by death. At the same time, to protect himself from Elizabeth's rage, he overlaid this bold action with conspicuous flattery. He named his first and only daughter, born that same year, Elizabeth.

Such attention to flattering details, plus lack of other strong contenders for the throne, brought James the English Crown. And along with James came two sons and a daughter—insurance against future problems of succession to the throne, if only he could settle for all time the legal doubts about his own succession.

However, his first problem was simply to stay alive. He arrived in London to find the city raging with plague. In a single year every family, rich or poor, had lost at least one member. Some 30,000 people had perished in a population of about 150,000.

All meetings, official or private, had to be canceled or postponed, thus giving James a dangerous taste of one-man rule for almost a year. Even the Puritans who presented their Millenary Petition—so named because it supposedly contained a thousand signatures—as James rode into London had to be put off until mid-January 1604. And Parliament was not called into session until two months after that.

As the plague subsided, James arranged to meet the Puritans, the nation's most conspicuous anti-Catholics. He invited their representatives to his favorite royal residence, old Henry VIII's Hampton Court Palace, fifteen miles by boat down the Thames River from the heart of London. Here, in distractingly lavish rooms, set amid acres of gardens and manicured trees, Dr. John Reynolds, England's leading scholar, and three Puritan ministers found themselves pitted against a much larger and decidedly hostile group. The Archbishop of Canterbury, supported by eight bishops and ten dignitaries of the Established English Church, had personal stakes in clinging to Anglicanism, Elizabeth's old compromise between Catholicism and Protestantism.

But James was Scottish, so felt no emotional ties to the English Church. At the very beginning, he stunned the bishops by referring to "your"—not "our" or even "my"—Established Church, despite his royal position as titular head. When the Puritans demanded that absolution be abolished, the King turned to face the Archbishop of Canterbury and his coterie: "I know not how it is used in your Church, but have heard it likened to the Pope's pardon."

Greatly encouraged, Dr. Reynolds urged abolition of every vestige of Catholicism in the official service, pointing particularly to the sign of the cross in baptism and use of the word *priest*. Infuriated, the bishops demanded that the King reject all compromise, change nothing. The King listened to everyone, occasionally interrupting with some lightly humorous remark. Sensing royal support, Dr. Reynolds went on to beg for simplified music and chants, "abridging the longsomeness of the service," greater strictness in keeping Sunday as a day of rest, and the encouragement of preaching.

Then the good Dr. Reynolds bumbled. Unthinkingly he used the word *presbytery* in proposing that the lower clergy be allowed to meet in conference and the bishop consult the *synod* of his diocese.

The King exploded. Remembering his misery and humiliation in Scotland and determined therefore to preserve intact his dual position as head of the English Church and State, James screamed at the Puritans, "If you aim at a Scottish Presbytery, it agrees as well with a monarchy as God and the Devil. Then Jack and Tom and Will and Dick shall meet, and at their pleasures censure me and my council. Stay, I pray you for seven years, before you demand that of me; and if then you find me pursy and fat, and my windpipe stuffed, I will perhaps hearken unto you. How they used the poor lady, my mother, is not unknown, and how they dealt with me in my minority. I thus apply it: No bishop, no king. Well, Dr. Reynolds, have you anything more to say?"

"No more, if it please your Majesty."

"If this be all your party has to say, I will make them conform themselves, or else harry them out of the land, or worse."

The Established Church had won. The Elizabethan settlement would remain: England would have Catholic ritual, but with the king at the head of the Church, instead of a foreign pope. Of course, the Puritans had never even contemplated separation of Church and State—an idea still in the distant future—but only that the Established Church should be Puritan, with less out-of-date ritual and more Renaissance emphasis on the individual. But they lost their argument, partly through

Dr. Reynolds's tactlessness, and partly because England had proved herself stronger than Spain, the Pope's military arm. The English monarchy no longer needed to buy the strong anti-Catholic support of the Puritans with special concessions.

Under these circumstances, this tumultuous conference yielded only one agreement—the decision to work on a new translation of the Bible, eventually published in 1611 as the King James Version, and universally considered a masterpiece.

Describing events at Hampton Court to a Scottish friend, James wrote that he had "peppered the Puritans soundly." Quite pleased with himself, he turned his attention to legalizing his succession to the throne. Jubilantly, Parliament cooperated, passing the Succession Act of 1604, subtitled "A most joyful and just recognition of the immediate, lawful, and undoubted Succession, Descent, and Right of the Crown."

Grateful to see James replace Elizabeth without a shattering civil war, Parliament gave "hearty thanks to Almighty God for blessing us with a Sovereign adorned with the rarest gifts of mind and body." Then marking the end of the state of alarm, they declared:

We, bound by the laws of God and man, do recognize and acknowledge that immediately upon the decease of Elizabeth, late Queen of England, the Imperial Crown of the realm of England, and of all the kingdoms, dominions, and rights belonging to the same, did by inherent birthright and lawful and undoubted succession descend and come to your most excellent Majesty, as being lineally, justly, and lawfully next and sole heir of this realm as is foresaid.

Once the succession was established, it was the King's Scottish upbringing and royal experience that gave him the most trouble, interfering with his English kingship at the very first meeting of Parliament. He was used to Scotland's Parliament—one House, unquestioningly subservient to an all-powerful king. Coming to England late in life (aged thirty-seven) and with firm habits of action, James completely overlooked the existence of two Houses—Lords and Commons—in the English Parliament. Nor was he prepared for their supreme self-assurance, bred from living in a settled and unified country, which prompted them to question, criticize, or even rebel against the King's pronouncements.

In England he barged into Parliament, making his opening address to the House of Lords, ignoring Commons completely. Commons remembered the insult, even though he did try to make amends three days later, as Edward Montague wrote in his private journal: "The King, most graciously, to satisfy the grief of the House, repeated his speech unto them. . . . This did notably please the House."

Leery of their new king, Commons decided that they must immediately instruct him on the workings of the English government. They explained: "Firstly, our privileges and liberties are our right and due inheritance, no less than our very lands and goods; secondly, they cannot be withheld from us, denied, or impaired, but with apparent wrong to the whole state of the realm."

Then they insisted that the King free from prison one of their members, Sir Thomas Shirley. And they demanded the seating of an outlaw, Sir Francis Goodwin, newly elected member from Buckinghamshire. The King yielded on Sir Thomas, but balked at a Parliamentary seat for an outlaw. Commons fought back, refusing to concede Goodwin's outlawry and insisting that he was lawfully elected. Anger on all sides, then compromise. Goodwin never took his seat, but neither did the King ever question again the right of Parlia-

Portrait of James I, by Daniel Mytens, 1621—Courtesy National
Portrait Gallery, London.

ment to judge the election returns of its members (a precedent taken to America, used in colonial legislatures, and in-
serted in the Constitution of the United States—Article I, Section 5: "Each house shall be the judge of the elections, returns
and qualifications of its own members.").

Reacting in the aftermath of the Shirley and Goodwin
cases, Commons scolded the King: "From these misinformed
positions, most gracious Sovereign, the greatest part of our
troubles, distrusts, and jealousies have risen."

Then they provided still more precedents to take to America. They pleaded for Parliamentary immunity from arrest
and for free speech for members: "The persons chosen, during the time of the Parliament as also of their access and recess,
shall be free from restraint, arrest, and imprisonment, and in
Parliament they may speak freely their consciences without
check and controlment." But James ignored this petition, em-
phasizing that he would look to royal precedent not to Parliament for guidance. No English monarch had ever granted
such privileges. Nor would he. (These privileges insisted on
by Parliament turned up in not so different words in the
United States Constitution, Article I, Section 6: "Senators and
Representatives shall . . . be privileged from arrest during
their attendance at the session of their respective Houses, and
in going to and returning from the same; and for any speech
or debate in either House, they shall not be questioned in any
other place.")

After four months of sessions the King had had enough of
insolence and lessons. In July 1604, he recessed Parliament.
Sarcastically addressing the House of Commons as "my Mas-
ters of the lower House" in his accompanying speech, he intoned his own veiled warning: "I wish you would use your
liberty with more modesty in time to come. You must know
that the Parliament not sitting, the liberties are not sitting. My

justice shall always sit in the same seat. Justice I will give to all, and favour to such as deserve it." Then in a friendlier tone he ended: "Take this with you for a conclusion, and believe it. That never king was more loving or thankful to a people, or more careful than I am to ease their burdens."

Within months, however, he contradicted his own final words by carrying out one of his first threats, made at the Hampton Court Conference, to make the Puritans "conform" or "harry them." He ordered Puritan ministers silenced and removed from their pulpits. The King might be a newcomer to English ways, but he quickly caught on to the use of pulpits for spreading news, opinions, and controversy. (Newspapers were still nonexistent.) Fifty Puritan ministers were removed, according to the official estimate of the Church of England. The Puritans put the number at three hundred, though historical research has now pegged it at closer to ninety. Whatever the numbers, this royal action frayed the cooperation between King and Parliament. Future combatants began choosing sides—the King supported by his bishops and nobles versus the Puritan middle class in Commons.

But then the badly bungled Gunpowder Plot of November 1605 intervened, winning a short reprieve for the King, and helping him to recoup some of his lost popularity. In an effort to destroy the King, Lords, and Commons with one massive explosion, fanatic Catholics had planned to dynamite Parliament on opening day of the second session. However, talkative conspirators exposed the plot, saved the government—and gave Englishmen an excuse for tremendous displays of fireworks and the burning in effigy of chief conspirator Guy Fawkes every November 5. During the year that followed, the camaraderie resulting from mutual danger of violent death and national anarchy made relations between James and Parliament uncommonly harmonious as they worked together to legislate extreme anti-Catholic measures and new taxes.

James desperately needed these new taxes. Before becoming king of Great Britain, he had dreamed of wealth and grandeur. And long after his coronation he stubbornly refused to accept the fact that he and England were almost bankrupt, thanks partly to Elizabeth's curious finances. For most of her forty-five-year reign the Queen had managed to avoid heavy taxation by extraordinary thrift, an austere court, and her practice of rewarding pirates with knighthoods. Sir Francis Drake, for example, won his title by plundering Spanish shipping, returning almost £2,000,000 in gold to the Queen after his trip around the world in the years 1577–1580. Also, the old Queen had saddled her successor with unpaid debts of £40,000.

Fortunately for James, Elizabeth bequeathed to him one of her best advisers, Robert Cecil, whom the King awarded with the earldom of Salisbury in 1605, and made Lord Treasurer in 1608. The "little beagle" as James affectionately nicknamed this hunchbacked old man, was the only adviser the King had who was able, English, and trained under Elizabeth. The other royal advisers were Scottish, knew nothing, and cared less about English politics. As the Scottish poet Alexander Craig brazenly chanted:

> We come from farthest Scottish coasts to thee,
> Some portion of thy royal feast to find:
> It rests in thee to welcome us therefore
> And make me rich, that I may beg no more.

James withstood volcanic financial pressure with Cecil's help. Actually, James's only responsibility for the shaky financial situation early in his reign arose from his failure to curb expenditures of a frivolous wife and an extravagant court.

By 1607 he had spent £92,000 on jewels, and had indulgently allowed his Queen, Anna of Denmark, to run up a bill of £40,000 to the goldsmith George Herriot alone. And by 1610 James bestowed £222,000 on fellow Scotsmen and some of the aristocracy. These sums were astronomical compared to the annual income of the average wealthy yeoman sitting in Commons at the beginning of James's reign— £400.

Other bills facing James resulted from foreign hostilities. He himself had brought to an end Elizabeth's nineteen-year war with Spain. But unpaid debts still remained from that conflict—which had included the final defeat of the Spanish Armada in 1588. Ongoing expenses included aid to the Netherlands to subsidize that country's war to break free of Spanish rule. The long process of subduing the Irish in order to colonize their country also required great sums of money.

Plundered gold was no longer available to England, after piracy was specifically forbidden in the 1604 peace treaty with Spain. And at the same time, Spanish gold and silver flowing into Europe from the West Indies was causing rampant inflation, disastrous for England, which had almost no overseas investment and so no compensating revenue. Money worth £4 in the early sixteenth century was worth scarcely £1 in the early seventeenth century.

Cecil as royal adviser had intimate knowledge of the English government, gained from working closely with Queen Elizabeth. He directed the King's attention to several effective schemes for raising money, with the result that by 1610 the national debt had returned to the level at which Elizabeth had left it. Customs duties ("tonnage and poundage") had been flowing into the royal treasury for three hundred years, granted automatically by Parliament at the beginning of each new reign for the duration of the kingship. More recently, the Tudors had begun granting monopolies, sole trading rights given to a person or group in return for payment of huge fees to the Crown. The same Tudor imagination had devised *Benevolences*, a poetic description for a monstrous practice—forced loans to the Crown whenever, wherever, on whomever, and for however long the monarch in his or her wisdom and generosity decided. On their own, James and Cecil invented the sale of titles, notably baronets, which carried with them admission to the House of Lords. The King benefited from the added wealth, but at the cost of weakening respect for the membership of the House of Lords, in comparison to Commons whose members had arrived through proven leadership.

In March 1610, when the King was no longer haunted by debt, he called Parliament into session to work out a permanent supply of money for the Crown, an income of £200,000 per year. By way of sweetening his request, he offered to give up several feudal practices that had long since decayed into corruption or oppression—and over which Parliament had no control. But Parliament refused to surrender any of what they considered their "ancient" power to levy taxes, unless the King gave them a much larger share in decision making.

Stung by their obstinacy, the King came back snarling. He transformed his God-given right to succeed to Elizabeth's throne (so innocently included by Parliament in the Succession Act of 1604) into his divine right to wield absolute power. To disobey the King would mean disobeying God: "Kings are justly called gods for that they exercise a manner of resemblance of divine power upon earth. . . . They make and unmake their subjects; they have power of raising and casting down; of life and of death; judges over all their subjects and in all causes, and yet accountable to none but God only. . . . As to dispute what God may do is blasphemy, so it is sedition in subjects to dispute what a king may do in height of his power. I will not be content that my power be disputed upon."

Parliament bristled, stubbornly reminding the King of the "ancient, general, and undoubted right of Parliament to debate freely all matters which do properly concern the subject and his right or state, which freedom of debate being once foreclosed, the essence of the liberty of Parliament is withal dissolved." On the floor of Parliament a member conceded "the regal power from God," but reminded the King that "the actuating thereof is from the people" (an idea soon to take root 3,000 miles over the sea in Massachusetts).

By July 7, 1610, Parliament retaliated with growing political sophistication. Commons produced a Petition of Grievances, specifically demanding that "all impositions [tariffs to regulate trade] set without the assent of Parliament may be quite abolished and taken away" and a law made to this effect. They enumerated their economic hardships brought about by the King's policies and warned of "the causing of a general dearth and decay of wealth among your people, who will be hereby no less discouraged than disabled to supply your Majesty when occasion shall require it."

The King fired back his response, picturing himself quite well able to function without Parliament. But Parliament ignored his implied threat. They thundered their insistence on reviving the ancient power of the purse strings. No concessions by the King, no appropriations or taxes voted by Parliament (another legislative device carried directly to America). The King settled for the only indisputable victory allowed to him. He dissolved Parliament.

The timing was disastrous. Within the year, death claimed the King's brilliantly resourceful adviser, Lord Treasurer Robert Cecil, and the popular young heir to the throne, Prince Henry. Ironically, the best known gossip and letter writer of

his time, John Chamberlain, had declared just a short time before their deaths that the then prevalent diseases "kill few of
the better sort." But by March 11, 1612, Chamberlain was
writing of Cecil: "His sickness drowned all other news. Every
man's care or curiosity ran that way, insomuch that it seems
he was never so well beloved as now when they thought him
near lost." And on May 27, Chamberlain had to announce Cecil's death after a "long, languishing sickness." Six months
later, Chamberlain's snobbery again backfired. Eighteen-year-
old Prince Henry, athletic and strong-appearing, returned
from a game of tennis and collapsed, fatally stricken by "none
other than the ordinary ague that has reigned and raged almost all over England since the later end of summer." The
Prince had attracted grateful public attention by threatening
to run off to Protestant Germany rather than marry a French
Catholic as his father had advised. Furthermore, he had continually urged the King to support exploration and settlement
of the New World.

The double tragedy of these deaths in 1612 affected the entire nation as much as James himself. Without the advice of
Cecil or the possibility of a well-endowed marriage for his
older son, Prince Henry, James found himself financially desperate. And England sank deeper into poverty, misery, and
drabness.

Out of grief for the death of her brother—whose last co-
herent words had been "Where is my dear sister?"—Princess
Elizabeth canceled all engagement parties and postponed for
three months her marriage to the Protestant German Prince
Frederick V. When the wedding finally took place on St.
Valentine's Day in 1613, the festivities almost bankrupted, but
at least brightened, a gloomy England. A gaily costumed procession wound its way around the center of London and the
royal palace of Whitehall. With great imagination and inspi-

ration someone had costumed the musicians to look like priests or Indians from England's first American colony in Virginia. Welcomed with as much surprise as national pride, America had seeped into English consciousness, giving life an added diversion.

"The Wisest Fool in Christendom"

With Cecil gone, King James decided to act as his own chief adviser. He luxuriated in his own claims of divinity.

Unfortunately, there was nothing godlike in his appearance, especially as he grew older. He had spindly bowed legs in an era when men's clothes emphasized the appearance of their legs. His doublets and breeches, heavily quilted against the danger of an assassin's knife, gave him the appearance of a roly-poly clown. Nor were his clothes ever changed "until worn out to very rags," his clerk of the kitchen, Anthony Weldon, noted. Worse, he had a tongue so big in his mouth that speech was difficult. And his eating habits were positively repulsive. Food dribbled out of the sides of his mouth, to be wiped off by filthy hands, which Weldon described as being soft as "taffeta sarsnet," because he never washed them, "only rubbed his finger ends slightly with the wet end of a napkin."

The King's personality matched his appearance. He was lazy, loved his pleasures, such as hunting, so much that he would at the slightest excuse drop his royal responsibilities, allowing court favorites to run the country. His outsized pride in his command of Latin grammar and vocabulary—he regularly conversed in Latin—soon became a ruse for foreign diplomats to win important points with him. Purposely they would make Latin errors so that James could exercise superiority in correcting them. And he insisted that courtiers use adulatory language in addressing him—"pleaseful, wise, learned, most sacred," etc.

Even his good points found few admirers. He was a great patron of gardens, gardeners, and gardening, but spent more time on this hobby than in learning the details of English history and government. "He was infinitely inclined to peace," remarked Anthony Weldon, "but more out of fear than conscience." He saw clearly the dangers of tobacco, and alienated some of his wealthy supporters who were hoping to reap a profit from overseas colonization. In 1604 he wrote a scholarly tract denouncing tobacco as "a custom loathsome to the nose, harmful to the brain, dangerous to the lungs, and in the black stinking fume thereof, nearest resembling the horrible Stygian smoke of the pit that is bottomless." Eight years later when tobacco became the Virginia colony's chief cash crop, he refused to recant but agreed to allow importation of Virginia tobacco into England and to put an embargo on Spanish tobacco. Similarly far in advance of his time—100 years— on another subject, he urged Parliament to legislate formal union between England and Scotland, but angered Parliament by making no provision to prevent the weakening or destruction of England's ancient laws. In the absence of Parliamentary legislation (which came finally in 1707), he defiantly proclaimed himself "King of Great Britain," and proceeded to use that title on official documents.

When statesmanship began to take too much time away from hunting, James turned for advice not to an Englishman, but to the twenty-six-year-old Scotsman Robert Carr—stupid, arrogant, and spectacularly handsome. The King made him Earl of Somerset, and kept him always in sight like a beautiful ornament—until the ugliest scandal of James's reign consumed him.

At Carr's insistence, James had put tremendous pressure on his bishops to allow Lady Frances Howard, with whom Carr had fallen in love, to divorce her husband in 1612. Two years later Carr and his bride were discovered to have poisoned to death Cecil's old Secretary of State, Sir Thomas Overbury, for his opposition to the marriage. Tried before the House of Lords, the Carrs were found guilty and sentenced to death, only to be pardoned by the King and exiled to live out their lives in the backcountry.

This was the unembroidered version of the story.

Gossipers added titillating tales of sorcery—all believable in an age that accepted witchcraft. Frances Howard, according to her own maids, had bewitched Carr into falling in love with her by using love potions. And she had come to the aid of the bishops in the divorce proceedings by casting spells over her unwanted husband. As for the King, he had substituted his formerly firm belief in witchcraft for reliance on outright intrigue. Told that the commission of ten, which he had appointed to approve the divorce, was about to split in a five-to-five tie, he argued in person before them for three hours. When he saw himself getting nowhere, he added two more bishops to the commission. He eked out a seven-to-five vote in his favor, but in the process shattered the royal court, shook confidence. in his own divinity—and judgment—and blemished the infallibility of the Established English Church.

The King exposed himself wallowing in tactlessness, dirty intrigue, and poor advice, while the Puritans secured their halos. Their man at court was the Archbishop of Canterbury,

the fifty-year-old distinguished Oxford theologian, George
Abbott. The King had recently appointed Abbott to top rank
in the Church, despite his well-known views bordering on
Puritanism. Now the new Archbishop occupied the highest
moral ground on behalf of the Puritans by standing firmly and
publicly against the divorce.

Before the scandal, James had leaned on Carr to the extent
of following his advice not to call a new Parliament. Instead,
the King had tried raising enough money by new schemes
such as a public lottery, sale of court lands, excessive fines in
the old Tudor court of the Star Chamber, and creating additional knighthoods. But he had no particular success, so decided to try to work with Parliament again.

Slyly, the King followed the Tudor practice of sending
courtiers into all counties to manage elections so as to insure
favorable action from Parliament. However, news of the
scheme leaked out, royal candidates were defeated, and the
King, not understanding that the Tudor century had passed
into history, self-righteously protested his innocence: "My
integrity is like the whiteness of my robe, my purity like the
metal of gold in my crown, my firmness and clearness like the
precious stones I wear, and my affections natural like the red-
ness of my heart."

The Parliament of 1614, which has since been given the
distinctive but insultingly descriptive name "The Addled Parliament," was full of "new men." Totally lacking in Parliamentary experience, they proved to be excellent representatives of the emerging social and economic classes of England.
Commons in particular was now drawing members from merchant classes beginning to profit from overseas trade and
New World ventures, and from the gentry, who added indus-
triousness and initiative to the spoils their grandfathers had
acquired from Henry VIII's dissolution of the Catholic

monasteries. Content in the late sixteenth century to receive crumbs of respect and prestige from Elizabeth, Commons in the seventeenth century began demanding a larger role in government at the expense of the King. For two months and two days they tried to outmaneuver the King, unanimously disputed his power of levying taxes without Parliamentary approval, and denounced severe treatment of Puritan nonconformists. But they lost out to the King, who forced their dissolution before they could pass a single piece of legislation. Except for this nine-week interval, James ruled without Parliament during the ten-year period extending from 1611 to 1621.

Always on the brink of personal tragedy or royal catastrophe, James managed to find another chief adviser, George Villiers. The King ignored the availability of Sir Francis Bacon, philosopher, scientist, and man of letters. He preferred beauty to brains. Writing some thirty years after Villiers's rise to power, royal historian Edward Hyde, First Earl of Clarendon, mocked Villier's career by focusing praise on his physical attractions:

> Never any man, in any age, nor, I believe, in any country,
> or nation, rose in so short a time to so much greatness
> of honour, fame, and fortune, upon no other advantage
> or recommendation than of the beauty and gracefulness
> and becomingness of his person.

In the spring of 1615, Villiers's career began with his appointment as a gentleman of the bedchamber. By 1616, he was a viscount, by 1617, the Earl of Buckingham and a privy councillor, and by 1618, at the age of twenty-six, the virtual ruler of England—a rise which Clarendon described as "so quick, that it seemed rather a flight than a growth." Sir Fran-

Duke of Buckingham
Courtesy National Portrait Gallery, London.

cis Bacon warned from the lower echelons as king's attorney general and Lord Keeper: "You are as a new risen star, the eyes of all men are upon you; let not your negligence make you fall like a meteor."

With his usual fondness for nicknames, James called his new and most favored favorite "Sweet Steenie" (a name derived from St. Stephen, described by his fellow, twelfth-century Englishman William of Malmesbury as "approachable, good looking, always cheerful in the Lord—everyone liked him"). The King allowed Villiers to put all his relatives in high office, to provide himself with at least £80,000 in gifts of land by 1617, and to exercise supreme power.

Together with Villiers, the King managed somehow to collect enough money to keep the country operating without summoning Parliament. English overseas trade, and thereby taxes collected in the form of customs duties, was growing. And a great deal of business was coming in from the East India Company founded in 1600.

England received an unexpected bonus with the sudden outbreak of the Thirty Years War in 1618, Catholic Europe's attempt to undo the Protestant Reformation. By remaining neutral and continuing to trade while the Continent bled, James and England profited economically for a year or two. Despite the pleas of Protestants at home and his impetuous twenty-one-year old German son-in-law that he should aid in the unique opportunity to demolish the Holy Roman Empire, founded on the Hapsburg-Spanish-Catholic alliance, James determined to remain aloof.

Meanwhile, James's daughter, Princess Elizabeth, continued to encourage her husband, even though her father as King of England would promise no help. She remarked that she "would rather eat sauerkraut as wife of a king than roast meat as wife of an elector [princeling]. In 1618 Frederick accepted the kingship of Bohemia, offered by German nobles in hopes of bringing England into the alliance against the Holy Roman Emperor Ferdinand II. Still James was unmoved. Frederick suffered disastrous defeat, and escaped with his family to live out his life in exile among the Dutch who, looking back on his few months' reign, dubbed him the "Winter King." He and his wife became footnotes to history, grandparents of George I of England and great-great-grandparents of George III who presided over the American Revolution.

James had long resisted calling Parliament to raise money, even when the plight of the Winter King frightened English Protestants with visions of Catholic invasion and conquest. He hated the prospect of having to bargain away any of his royal powers in return for loosening Parliament's hold on the purse strings. But by 1621 he no longer had any choice except to summon Parliament. A disastrous economic depression had hit England, striking especially hard at the cloth industry, long England's main hope for future prosperity. Significantly, there was a three-way link here—from the cloth industry, to Puritanism, to Parliament. The industry centered in Essex, Suffolk, and Norfolk, which were eastern English counties full of Puritans who looked to their fellow sympathizers in Parliament for immediate political help.

The King was sick, Parliament was hostile, and abrupt dissolution was a constant threat. Crises erupted in rapid succession, the first when Parliament accused Sir Francis Bacon, now James's Lord Chancellor, of crimes against the nation. They leveled specific charges of bribery against Sir Francis. The King insisted on his right to try his minister before a special commission, selected by the King. Commons refused, successfully demanding that the King's ministers be tried before the House of Lords and be dismissed if found guilty. Bacon confessed to bribery, but not before Commons had indelibly as-

serted the responsibility of ministers to Parliament, instead of
to the monarch alone as under the Tudors.

With no master plan or grand design, Parliament moved
still further from the Tudor era in the next round of crises.
The King's need for money emboldened members to claim
rights that Parliament had never had under Elizabeth—rights
to involvement in religious and foreign affairs, plus the privilege of freedom of speech in Parliamentary debate. Several
times during the month of December 1621, they petitioned
the King, only to receive negative responses telling them: "I
am an old and experienced King needing no such lesson." Or
directing them to admit that their "privileges were derived
from the grace and permission of our ancestors and us."

The angry reaction of Parliament made the King tone
down his strong words, but not enough to satisfy Commons,
which dropped all other business for a week while they produced the Great Protestation, carefully restating their position:

> That the liberties, franchises, privileges, and jurisdic-
> tions of Parliament are the ancient and undoubted birth-
> right and inheritance of the subjects of England; and that
> the arduous and urgent affairs concerning the King, State,
> and defense of the realm, are proper subjects and matter
> of counsel and debate in Parliament; and that in the han-
> dling and proceeding of those businesses every member of
> the House of Parliament has, and of right ought to have,
> freedom of speech to propound, treat, reason, and bring
> to conclusion the same.

Furious, James tore the page containing the Protestation
from the record of Parliamentary proceedings, and imprisoned
four leaders—again ignoring Parliament's self-proclaimed free-

dom of speech. Then abruptly he dissolved Parliament.

Among the four imprisoned was sixty-four-year-old Sir Edward Coke, whom the King had earlier fired unceremoniously for open defiance. Brilliant champion of the common law (law based on court decisions, tradition, and custom), Coke had had the audacity to publicize his own belief that courts had to be independent of the Crown. Looking more royal than the King with his white moustache and goatee, and tall, thin figure, Coke (pronounced Cook) had claimed the right for judges to decide disagreements between King and Parliament. As far back as July 1610, responding to a petition from Parliament, he and his fellow justices had issued what English constitutional historian J. R. Tanner called "one of the minor charters for English liberty": "That the King by his proclamation cannot create any offense which was not an offense before, for then he may alter the law of the land by his proclamation in a high point, for if he may create an offense where none is, upon that ensues fine and punishment." In other words, a person cannot be convicted of a crime committed yesterday in the name of a law passed today.

The King at first ignored Coke, then angrily dismissed him for handing down legal decisions contrary to royal positions. With supreme inconsistency—or senility—James allowed Coke to enter Commons in 1621, where he played a leading role in both the proceedings against his arch rival, Sir Francis Bacon, and in drawing up the Great Protestation. James's reaction to Coke's Parliamentary maneuvers was to throw him into the Tower of London for almost seven months. But when Parliament again reconvened—in 1624—Coke reappeared.

As James grew older, and progressively less responsible, sometimes momentous constitutional developments occurred almost frivolously. Thanks to two easily detectable disguises —black beards pasted on the chins of the King's chief minister

George Villiers (to whom the King now gave pretensions of royalty by naming him the Duke of Buckingham) and the King's son and heir, Prince Charles—James's last Parliament of 1624 won its long struggle to discuss foreign policy. Buckingham had convinced James that peace overtures to Spain would return the kingship of Bohemia to his son-in-law, the Winter King. And so the King authorized Buckingham and Charles—alias "Tom and Dick Smith"—to race through Europe in their false beards to claim the hand of the Spanish Infanta for Charles. They all hoped that in addition to settling the Bohemian question, the negotiations would produce a large dowry, enabling Charles to rule without Parliament when he succeeded to the throne. But Spain refused to allow Charles even to see the Infanta, let alone propose marriage. One high Spanish official proclaimed publicly: "We would rather put the Infanta headlong into a well than into his hands."

Humiliated, James and his last Parliament in 1624 agreed to war on the high seas against Catholic Spain. James asserted: "I promise you, on the word of a King, that although war and peace be the peculiar prerogative of kings, yet as I have advised with you in the treaties on which war may ensue, so I will not treat nor accept of a peace without first acquainting you with it and hearing your advice, and therein go the proper way of Parliament in conferring and consulting with you in such great and weighty affairs."

The Parliament of 1624 won several other major victories, some with the active connivance of Prince Charles and Buckingham—despite the old King's flash of foresight: "You are making a rod with which you will be scourged yourself." First, in the area of foreign policy, Parliament won not only the right to debate and advise, but to appropriate money to be used under strict Parliamentary supervision. Second, it firmly established the constitutional precedent of impeachment when it impeached and ruined Lord Treasurer Lionel Cranfield, Earl of Middlesex—who, unlike Bacon, pleaded "not guilty" and went to trial. (With this, old James let fly another of his Cassandralike warnings: "You will live to have your bellyful of impeachments.") Last, this Parliament succeeded in passing legislation to confine the hated granting of monopolies to new inventions only. The King's death, on March 27, 1625, interrupted Parliament's most successful constitutional confrontation with the monarchy.

James's arrogance, vanity, and foreignness combined to make him a less than ordinary ruler at a time when England required an extraordinary, superhuman king. While trade and industrialism were strengthening the middle class and bursting through the remains of a feudal society that had kept everyone in his place, James as King increased rather than solved his country's problems. His subterfuges, which had allowed him to rule largely without Parliament, meant that no new laws on any subject were enacted between 1610 and 1624. His attempts at absolute rule resulted instead in a leaderless anarchy mixed with periods of economic chaos.

Two of James's contemporaries who survived to write about him after his death were most uncomplimentary. Arthur Wilson (1595–1652), gentleman-in-waiting to the third Earl of Essex during the reign of James and later author of three plays, wrote: "He was born a King and from that height, the less fitted to look into inferior things." Another writer, Sir Anthony Weldon, James's former clerk of the kitchen whom he knighted in 1617, quoted a "very wise man" as saying of King James: "He was the wisest fool in Christendom, meaning him wise in small things, but a fool in weighty affairs."

During his lifetime James had been subject of a satire performed on the London stage, the first time in history anyone had dared to satirize a reigning English king.

And treasonously hiding behind the name Tom Tell Troath, an anonymous writer circulated his letter telling the King: "All parties make a mock of your words 'Great Britain.' They offer to prove that GREAT BRITAIN is a great deal less than *little* England was wont to be: less in reputation, less in strength, less in riches, less in all manner of virtue."

With mocking gratitude two hundred years later, Parliamentary sympathizer and historian Thomas Babington Macaulay acknowledged: "If James's administration had been able and splendid, it would probably have been fatal to our country. We owe more to his weaknesses and meannesses than to the wisdom and courage of much better sovereigns."

Another historian, David Hume, found that at least one momentous development had occurred in the first quarter of the seventeenth century. In 1754, when the American colonies were adding to the glory and wealth of England, Hume wrote: "What chiefly renders the reign of James memorable is the commencement of the English colonies in America; colonies established on the noblest footing that has been known in any age or nation."

Simultaneously, then, this first Stuart king managed to set the stage for further constitutional confrontation with Parliament and for English colonization overseas. He left behind a war with Spain requiring generous financial support, and a Parliament willing to grant money only in return for a greater share in the government. At a time when settlers were needed to nail down Elizabethan claims in America, James bequeathed to his son an atmosphere of social and political discontent that would provoke Englishmen into abandoning their familiar homes for colonization in a world and an England that would both be "New."

"Their Chamber Pots Are Pure Gold"

On his voyage around the world, during the years 1577–1580, Francis Drake discovered New England—somewhere in what is now California.* It took two more generations for Englishmen to move New England 3,000 miles closer to old England and to plant permanent colonies there.

England was very nonchalant about overseas exploration throughout most of the sixteenth century. She had entered the race promisingly enough in 1497, a little more than five years after turning down Columbus's offer to sail for England instead of for Spain. A Venetian navigator Giovanni Caboto changed his name to John Cabot, took up residence in

---

* Almost fifteen hundred years before, the Roman historian Pliny had dubbed England *Albion*, in reference to the traveler's first view of the country, the White Cliffs of Dover. Sighting "the white banks and cliffs which lie towards the sea and noting the country's possible affinity with our country in name, which sometime was so called," Drake called his find *Nova Albion* or New England.

Bristol, a port in western England, and convinced England's new King Henry VII to authorize his voyage. Sailing his little ship *Matthew*, Cabot and his son Sebastian with a crew of eighteen became the first Europeans to set foot on the continent of North America, since the Northmen's voyages almost five centuries earlier. They landed somewhere around present-day Labrador or Newfoundland. On a second voyage, early in May 1498, Cabot went as far south as Cape Cod and Chesapeake Bay. England's claim to all of North America east of the Rockies and north of Florida rested on Cabot's voyages. (More than a century would pass before France staked out a strong, competing claim—New France, a permanent settlement in Quebec, Canada, fathered by Samuel de Champlain in 1608.)

Then, except for a lone voyage by Sebastian Cabot to northern North America in 1509, Englishmen stayed on their own little island until the middle of Elizabeth's reign. The land of North America seemed too poor and too far off at a time when England was threatened by domestic upheaval and foreign invasion. The Tudors first had to consolidate their rule against rebellious noblemen, and then unite, stabilize, and fortify their homeland before competing in the search for "Glory, God, and Gold."

By the 1580s, deadly rivalry between Spain and England erupted into war. Stakes included the supremacy of Catholicism or Protestantism, prestige and power in the world—both Old and New—and the vast riches waiting overseas. Piracy at first provided a temporary stopgap for England in the struggle, but plundered gold was secondhand, dangerous to obtain, and spasmodic in delivery.

Just a few years before the actual outbreak of war between the two nations, Queen Elizabeth granted a momentous charter to thirty-nine-year-old Humphrey Gilbert, newly knighted for his services in attempting to subdue Ireland. Elizabeth gave written, though vaguely worded, permission to Sir Humphrey "to discover remote, heathen and barbarous lands not actually possessed of any Christian prince or people and the same to have, hold, occupy and enjoy." Then, changing English colonization forever, she made the pronouncement that every Englishman traveling with Sir Humphrey "shall, and may, have and enjoy all privileges of free inhabitants and persons native of England, and within our allegiance." In addition, since living in such remote lands would make it "necessary for the safety of all men that adventure in those journeys and voyages to determine to live together in Christian peace and civil quietness each with the other, we do grant to Sir Humphrey full power and authority to govern and rule according to such statutes, laws and ordinances as near as conveniently may be agreeable to the form of the laws and policy of England." Henceforth, once an Englishman always an Englishman—complete with oft-proclaimed English rights, privileges, and duties.   ￼

But first England had to trounce Spain, mistress of Europe, the high seas, and America. In the war between Spain and England, both countries avoided using their homeland as battleground, fighting instead in the Netherlands, a Protestant country in the process of breaking away from Spanish Catholic rule. Stalemate set in. Then came the summer of 1588. With a well-placed assist from some of Nature's worst storms at sea, the English navy shattered and scattered the awesome Spanish Armada. Afterward, though the war dragged on for the rest of Elizabeth's reign, England increased in strength as Spain weakened.

With perfect timing, Richard Hakluyt appeared on the scene to construct the intellectual foundation for English exploration and exploitation of the New World. As the first professor of modern geography at Oxford University, he devoted thirty-two years, 1584–1616, to writing thousands of pages about the New World.

Hakluyt forecast vast economic rewards by opening an overseas market for England's woolen industry and for the sale of English-made "hats, bonnets, knives, fishhooks, copper kettles, beads, looking glasses, bugles, and a thousand kind of other wrought wares." Cannily, he pointed out that these exports would give "employment to many of our poor, who would otherwise starve or become burdensome." In return, England could import cheaply a long list of luxuries: "wood, salt, oil, wine, oranges, figs, pomegranates, rice, raw silks and dyes." And a shipbuilding industry, based on all sorts of otherwise unused woods such as "oak, cedar, pine and walnut," would not only give work to Englishmen but add ships to the navy, which, by "the navigating of the seas in the voyage, and of the great rivers there, will breed many mariners for service, and maintain much navigation."

Best of all, Hakluyt promised, Spain would be cut to size by "our planting in those parts and joining with those savages, their neighbors in Florida, and on the north side of Nova Hispaniola." He counted on support from disloyal Spanish subjects. Describing Spain's control of her colonies by a tyrannical government thousands of miles away in Madrid, he wrote: "People kept in subjection desire nothing more than freedom." Then he added, writing with the poetry that turned his tracts from mere propaganda into England's greatest prose epics:

And like as a little passage given to water makes its own way, so give but a small means to those kept in tyranny, and they will make their own way to liberty. . . . The Spanish empire will fall to the ground, and the Spanish king shall be left bare as Aesop's proud crow, the parrot, the popinjay; and every other bird, having taken home from him his gorgeous feathers, he will in short space become a laughing stock for all the world.

Exactly one year after publication of Hakluyt's introductory book, Sir Humphrey Gilbert's more famous half brother, Sir Walter Raleigh, attempted to plant England's first colony in America, at Roanoke Island, Virginia (the Latin name given to the whole Atlantic coastline north of Spanish Florida by Elizabeth herself). Three times between 1585 and 1587, he sent out expeditions (while he remained at home), spending the lavish sum of £40,000 hoping to establish a large feudal estate where he could be lord of the manor. The final and most serious attempt was made by 117 men, women, and children, who fatally chose to inhabit land that was the site of a huge Indian population, not at all anxious to share their meager supply of food. A search party sent to find survivors in 1590 turned back to England in the wake of a destructive storm at sea, convinced that no white man or woman could have survived in Virginia.

The loss of these colonists dampened enthusiasm for colonization—until time dimmed memories. Then during Elizabeth's last year on the throne, 1602, and throughout the reign of King James, 1603–1625, interest and activity in overseas expansion surged.

Adventure, nonconformity, and fish provided the spurs. In 1602, Bartholomew Gosnold, an assistant in Sir Walter Raleigh's attempt to colonize Roanoke, became the first European to establish a home in the area called Northern Virginia (New England today). Financed by Shakespeare's patron, the Earl of Southampton, and other wealthy noblemen, he departed from Bristol in western England. Sailing a straight course across the Atlantic, instead of the usual southern route from the Canary Islands, he arrived at modern-day Salem, Massachusetts. He then sailed on around a hook of land through waters so filled with cod that he dubbed it Cape Cod. And cod, he soon learned, substituted quite profitably for gold. Catholic Europe—most of Europe still practiced Catholicism—set up a great demand for codfish, which could be imported cheaply, after being salted and flaked to last indefinitely.

Cod first drew Gosnold and his crew to Northern Virginia. Once there, they found an abundance of fruit, wood, fur, and sassafras—an herb reputed to cure the French pox, plague, and many other serious illnesses. All these resources made the idea of permanent settlement highly attractive, exactly as Hakluyt had predicted. No matter that the land was already inhabited. The native Indians seemed to welcome the Englishmen, happily trading furs, hemp, copper, pipes, and tobacco, in return for knives, hatchets, and trifling gewgaws.

Soon, however, constant contact turned initial curiosity into mutual suspicion. Two of Gosnold's crew came under Indian attack, barely escaping with their lives. The entire crew made an immediate decision to set sail for England.

In 1605, the Earl of Southampton subsidized still another exploration of the same general area. This time Captain George Weymouth, a veteran of two previous Atlantic voyages seeking a northwest passage to Asia, led the expedition. He returned to England after several months, publicly displaying five live Indians. He considered them a great advertisement for the New World, plus proof that the natives there needed to be taught the language and civilization of the white man.

While efforts to colonize in the North continued, the next major attempt at English settlement shifted back to the South's

warmer climate and more fertile ground. The name of Gosnold became associated once again with Southern Virginia,
this time joined with the soon-famous John Smith.

Excitement over the well-advertised proposal to plant a
colony produced a satire written by Shakespeare's friend and
rival playwright, Ben Jonson, in coauthorship with John Marston and George Chapman. Designed for gentle ridicule, the
comedy became wildly successful on stage, starting with its
first production in 1605, and finally enticing King James himself to the theater on January 25, 1614. A contemporary even
asserted that Shakespeare himself played one of the leads that
night.

The authors named their satire *Eastward Ho!*, referring to
the idea that Columbus had discovered the East. And they
peopled the play with characters named Spendall, Scape
Thrift, Quicksilver, and Seagull. The audience loved Seagull's
description of Virginia:

> Gold is more plentiful there than copper is with us. All
> their dripping pans and chamber pots are pure gold. And
> all the chains with which they chain up their streets are
> solid gold. For rubies and diamonds they go forth on holi-
> days and gather them by the sea-shore to hang on their
> children's coats, and stick in their children's caps.

Seagull painted an Edenesque picture of the land where
the climate is "temperate and full of all sorts of excellent
viands" and then completed his paradisical description with
the English dream of freedom and upward mobility:

> You shall live freely there, without sergeants, or cour-
> tiers, or lawyers, or intelligencers. Then for your means
> to advancement, there it is simple, and not preposterously

mixed. You may be an alderman there, and never be a scavenger; you may be any other officer, and never be a slave.

Enthusiasm for the Virginia plantation translated itself into money, contributed at the rate of £12 10s. per share by small investors including both laymen and churchmen, wealthy men such as nobles and knights, middle-class merchants, and trade guilds. Balladeer Michael Drayton composed the merry "Ode to the Virginian Voyage" to honor the sailing of 144 colonists in three tiny ships on December 20, 1606:

> You brave heroic minds,
> Worthy your country's name,
>   That honour still pursue
>   Go, and subdue,
> Whilst loit'ring hinds
> Lurk here at home with shame.
>
> Britains, you stay too long,
> Quickly aboard bestow you,
>   And with a merry gale
>   Swell your stretch'd sail
> With vows as strong
> As the winds that blow you.
>
> And cheerfully at sea,
> Success you still entice,
>   To get the pearl and gold
>   *And ours to hold*
> VIRGINIA
> Earth's only Paradise.

Lack of experience in planting a colony, underlined by expectation of get-rich-quick profits, almost proved fatal to the Virginia venture. Mere survival sapped all the settlers' energy during the first crucial years. Food was scarce, a malaria epidemic killed half the colonists—including Bartholomew Gosnold—and hostile Indians continually conducted raids against the newcomers. In the second year, chances of success improved when John Smith became governor, displaying heroic organization, resourcefulness, and periodic tongue-lashing: "He that will not work, neither shall he eat." Finally, in 1612, John Rolfe gave the colony a marketable crop, tobacco. Still progress was slow, and by 1616, ten years after the first sailing to Virginia, the white population was only 351.

In 1619, the colony took three path-setting steps: (1) the importation of one hundred "young and uncorrupt" girls forcibly put aboard ship to be wives and breeders; (2) the establishment of the House of Burgesses, the first legislative assembly in North America; and (3) the purchase of twenty black African slaves from the Dutch.

At the same time, Spain, which had long threatened to destroy the Virginia colony, concluded that the English would undoubtedly go broke there without any help or hindrance, and that therefore the best course would be to waste no men, arms, or time in subduing the uninvited settlers.

In 1622 an Indian massacre—400 out of a finally thriving colonial population of 1240 were killed—plus bad and insufficient food, internal dissension, and lack of financial support from London led John Chamberlain to write that solving the Virginia colony's problems had become a "thorny business." King and Privy Council had to take over management of the colony from the near-bankrupt Virginia Company of London, finally revoking the charter in 1625. Virginia became

England's first royal colony directly (as far as possible at a distance of 3,000 miles) supervised by the King.

Admirers of that restless adventurer John Smith have enthusiastically speculated on a different outcome if their hero had chosen to remain in Virginia for longer than two and a half years. But Smith never really settled down until old age crept in. And then he busied himself writing an autobiography, which turned out to be literally fabulous. For example, he described his capture and sale into slavery to the charming and "noble gentlewoman" Charatza Tragabigzanda, when as a young soldier he fought the Turks in Transylvania and Hungary. And he told of his escape with her help in a story remarkably similar to the familiar tale of his later escape from the Virginia Indians, aided by chief Powhatan's daughter Pocahontas.

In June 1615, when Smith's captor was a less glamorous French pirate ship, he whiled away his enforced inactivity writing a detailed book about his exploration of New England. He had gone there on an earlier voyage in 1614 on behalf of Sir Ferdinando Gorges, a prominent member of the newly chartered Virginia Company of Bristol, "to take whales and make trials of a mine of gold and copper." During this exploration he had drawn what he described as "a map from point to point, isle to isle, and harbor to harbor, with the soundings, sands, rocks and landmarks," and called the area New England—the name suggested by Drake's "Nova Albion"—to replace the less accurate Northern Virginia, and to make the claim for England in America, alongside New Spain and New France. This map, by and large accurate, had an immediate advantage over others, which were more accurate but not for sale. John Smith's map was actually published and became widely available. Besides, Smith caught popular attention with all his extra drawings—a self-portrait, birds, beasts,

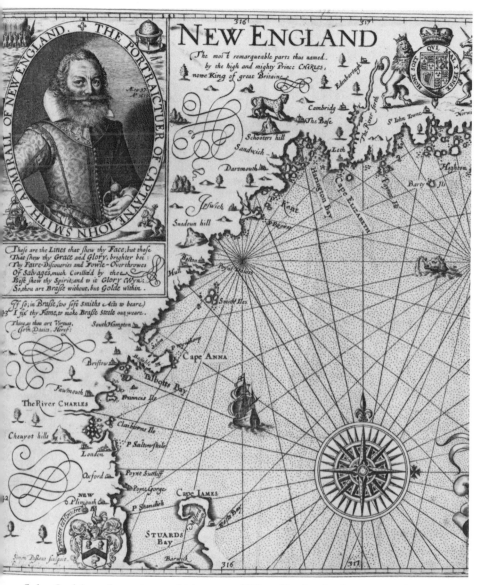

John Smith and portions of his map of New England—Courtesy of the Trustees of the British Museum, London.

sea monsters and ships.

Displaying great promotional talent, Smith enthused over New England in his book *A Description of New England:* "And of all the four parts of the world that I have yet seen not inhabited, could I have but means to transport a colony, I would rather live here than anywhere." Then he told his oppressed countrymen what they most wanted to know:

> And here are no hard landlords to rack us with high rents, or extorted fines to consume us; no tedious pleas in law to consume us with their many years' disputations for justice; no multitudes to occasion such impediments to good orders as in popular states. So freely have God and His Majesty bestowed those blessings on them that will attempt to obtain them as here every man may be master and own labor and land—or the greatest part—in a small time. If he have nothing but his hands, he may set up this trade, and by industry quickly grow rich, spending but half that time well which in England we abuse in idleness, worse, or as ill.

For those readers not yet convinced by the promise of liberty, land, and freedom from oppression, Smith wrote of the healthy climate, noting that of twenty-five men only two became ill there and they were "many years diseased before they went." Then he listed the natural resources: "victual to feed us, wood of all sorts to build boats, ships or barks, the fish at our doors, pitch, tar, masts, yams, and most of other necessaries only for taking."

After his escape from the French pirates, Smith—crowned with the hollow title Admiral of New England, by the Virginia Company of Bristol—shrewdly dedicated his manuscript to the fifteen-year-old heir to the throne, Prince Charles. He urged the young prince to please himself by changing any of the "alien" names. Thus, exotic Cape Tragabigzanda, named after John Smith's Turkish ladylove, became plain old Cape Ann in honor of the Queen, Charles's mother. Charles considered Indian names positively barbarous, and so changed Sawocatuck to Ipswich, Passtaquack to Hull, and Accomack to Plymouth. He named the Charles River after himself, a name that has persisted, and tried renaming Cape Cod for his father James, a name that did not take.

John Smith's paeans to New England may or may not have caught the attention of the community of some 238 Englishmen living in self-exile at Leyden, Holland. They had been there since 1608, harried out of the land by King James, exactly as he had threatened at Hampton Court in 1604. This was the group known by three different names depending on the attitude of the speaker. Their leader and longtime governor, William Bradford, loved them and first coined the name Pilgrims. Those who held them in contempt called them Brownists, after Robert Browne, who in 1580 had set up his own autonomous congregation because he was too impatient to wait for reformation of the Church of England. To King James and his court they were Separatists, whose initial departure from England had been a relief, since they refused to compromise their radical belief in complete independence from government in religious matters.

Many of the English exiles at Leyden had become disenchanted with their new home and were actively looking around for another place to settle. They complained that the Dutch were barring Englishmen from membership in the Leyden guilds, and thus they could find no jobs. In addition, they looked in horror at their children who knew little of English life or language. The final straw, in Bradford's words, was "the great licentiousness of youth" in Holland. The Dutch observed the Sabbath very casually, encouraging their children to indulge in lavish feasts and merrymaking. The contrast with their own strict demands for an entirely holy Sabbath was too much.

Even so, only 35 members of the Leyden church were willing to abandon Holland. The high death rate in Virginia, and fear of shipwreck or death at sea discouraged most of them from becoming pilgrims to America. (To their horror they had just learned of Blackwell, an Amsterdam elder, on whose ship bound for Virginia, 130 out of 180 had died.) In the end, the 35 from Leyden were joined by 66 from London and Southampton aboard the overcrowded, underprovisioned *Mayflower*, as the ship sailed from Plymouth, England, on September 16, 1620.

At this point history veers off into tantalizing mystery. What was the actual destination of the Pilgrims? Were they or were they not influenced by John Smith's writings? The current catechism has it that (1) the Pilgrims dismissed Virginia as being too Anglican, with an already established government, which might be no more receptive to their separatism than the government of England; (2) the land around the Hudson they considered seriously, despite Holland's claims there, based on exploration by Henry Hudson, who though an Englishman, had made the voyage for the Dutch; but (3) tremendous waves kept their fifty-year-old Captain Christopher Jones—an excellent and cautious seaman and one of the three owners of the *Mayflower*—from attempting to round Cape Cod, the first American land sighted. Thus, (4) on November 9, 1620, they beached at Cape Cod, which they could recognize from John Smith's map, with a patent that was invalid, because they had anchored some 200 miles north of their legal limit as defined by the King.

While still aboard ship they drew up and signed on November 21, 1620, the Mayflower Compact, the first written statement by English colonists that they intended to make their own laws. Bradford explained in his journal, *Of Plymouth Plantation, 1620–1647*, that the decision was

> occasioned partly by the discontented and mutinous speeches that some of the strangers [Non-Separatists] amongst them had let fall from them in the ship to the effect that when they came ashore they would use their own liberty, for none had power to command them, the patent they had being for Virginia and not for New England, which belonged to another government.

The Compact contains 199 words, 80 of them devoted to cream-puff introductory and closing formalities surrounding a highly significant 119-word sentence:

> Having undertaken, for the Glory of God and advancement of the Christian Faith and Honour of our King and Country, a Voyage to plant the First Colony in the Northern Parts of Virginia, we do by these presents solemnly and mutually in the presence of God and one of another, Covenant and Combine ourselves together into a Civil Body Politic, for our better ordering and preservation and furtherance of the ends aforesaid; and by virtue hereof to enact, constitute and frame such just and equal Laws, Ordinances, Acts, Constitutions and Offices, from time to time, as shall be thought most meet and convenient for the general good of the Colony, unto which we promise all due submission and obedience.

Forty-one adults signed the compact, including nineteen from Leyden, sixteen Londoners, four servants, and two sailors. Those not invited to sign were sick, underage, or women.

Americans generally revere Plymouth Colony for its unique contribution to local color—Thanksgiving—while students of government rhapsodize over the Mayflower Compact. Here is rare, written evidence of the political mythology born in ancient Greece 2,000 years before, and transported to America by English religious nonconformists.

The Mayflower Compact looked back to two legendary contracts. The first was made with God. He would carry out promises revealed in the Scriptures, in return for human obedience, repentance, and faith. To enforce this first contract, a second agreement had to be made, this time among the people themselves. They would create a government here on earth that would replace the lawless, cannibalistic state of nature, where they could not possibly live up to their original promises to God.

This seventeenth-century, mythlike retelling of how politics all began was shared with Puritans and Calvinists everywhere. After extensive use and refinement, compact theory found its way into the eighteenth-century United States Declaration of Independence and Constitution. By the twentieth century it was the unspoken hypothesis underlying modern representative government based on the consent of the governed.

After signing the Mayflower Compact on board ship, and exploring the local area in their tiny shallop for several weeks, the Pilgrims chose Plymouth for permanent settlement. With no great enthusiasm or mention of anchoring on Plymouth Rock, Bradford explained their choice. On Monday, December 21, 1620,

> they sounded the harbor and found it fit for shipping and
> found divers cornfields and little running brooks, a place

(as they supposed) fit for situation. At least it was the best they could find, and the season and their present necessity made them glad to accept of it.

Bradford called the Plymouth Colony's first year "the starving time." All but four of the one hundred two passengers had survived the voyage, but by the summer of 1621, only forty-eight remained alive. Very few of the women survived, including Bradford's wife, Dorothy. She is thought to have committed suicide, her spirit broken by long brutal weeks aboard the *Mayflower*, which reeked with the stench of human waste, her mind shattered by the sight of the frozen, empty land.

By 1626, six years after settlement, the population of Plymouth Colony was three hundred persons, and five years later in 1632, it had added two hundred more. By the end in 1691, when the colony was absorbed into Massachusetts Bay, it numbered no more than eight thousand, scattered in several towns. From start to finish it remained a settlement of humble men and women in terms of numbers, wealth, and education.

The Plymouth Colony bequeathed to later generations a stubbornness in pursuit of successful colonization and in opposition to the King's attempts to make them conform. There had been no one to assist them in the beginning as would have happened in Virginia. Bradford himself commented that there were "no friends to welcome them, no inns to entertain them or refresh their weatherbeaten bodies, no houses, or, much less, towns to repair to, to seek for succour." They had no wealth of their own and little financial support from London merchants, nor did Plymouth ever succeed in obtaining a charter from the King, which would make their settlement legally valid.

Furthermore, the Pilgrims had arrived, knowing in advance

as Bradford wrote, "the continual danger of the savage people, who are cruel, barbarous, and most treacherous." Some of the settlers angered the native Indians from time to time, using their crops, entering their wigwams uninvited, and helping themselves to handmade items. And some attacked and killed Indians as a means of preventing attacks on the colony. For the first fifty years, however, mutual noninterference generally marked relations between natives and newcomers, occasionally interspersed with cordiality, as when Indians taught Englishmen to plant corn, or when trade profitable to both parties was conducted, or when Indians acted as interpreters or guides.

The motivation for the Plymouth Colony had been not adventure or riches, but attainment of a divine heaven. Sir Ferdinando Gorges (an Italian-sounding first name was a popular affectation of the day among wealthy Englishmen), a staunch supporter of Church, king, and himself, had completely opposite motives for colonization. Hoping to add to his family's wealth and important connections, he had shown interest in the first attempt to settle the Maine coast in 1607. And in 1614 he had encouraged John Smith's exploration of New England. By 1620 he had organized several of his aristocratic friends into the Council for New England. The group sponsored about a dozen fishing or colonizing ventures along the New England coasts, between the years 1620 and 1624, none successful.

At about the same time, in 1623, a group calling itself the Dorchester Adventurers (men who risked or "adventured" capital in a business project), led by the Dorchester preacher John White and a group of wealthy West-Country English Puritans, obtained a charter to establish a colony on Cape Ann. The highly profitable fishing there, they reasoned, would be best protected by permanent inhabitants. But they could not convince the "colonists" to raise their own food supplies or to endure another New England winter, shivering in icy gale winds and frequently separated from the earth itself by mounds of snow. So the attempt failed.

At the time of King James's death in 1625, then, New England had been thoroughly explored and advertised, and at least one tiny settlement, Plymouth, had finally taken hold there. Virginia, on the other hand, was still reeling from the Indian massacre of 1622. Still, the Puritan middle class watched, waited, and remained in old England, a gloomier place than ever before—ravaged by plague, war, starvation, depression, and oppressive politics. The Puritans, however, saw themselves as no worse off than the rest of Europe. In fact, with the coming accession to the throne of Prince Charles, the country might have great good fortune. Unlike his father James, young Charles had lived most of his life in England. Surely as king he would understand and restore Parliament's rightful powers.

"Evil and Declining Times"

King Charles arrived for his official coronation dressed in white to symbolize his marriage to the people of England—and to divert attention from his sixteen-year-old bride's rebellion against the Protestant ceremony.

His Catholic Queen, Henrietta Maria, sister of Louis XIII of France, refused even to hide behind the grille in Westminster Abbey, where a place had been carefully prepared so that she could see the crowning of her husband. Instead, she sullenly watched the simple ceremony—Charles had defied tradition, rejecting the vulgar display of an elaborate procession—from a window of the Old Palace in the company of her French ladies-in-waiting. As always, Charles had the Duke of Buckingham at his side, promoted to the ancient office of Lord High Constable for this occasion.

The Queen's attitude incensed Charles. Angrily he complained to Buckingham of her "many little neglects," such as "eschewing to be in my company," and "her neglect of the English tongue and of the nation in general." Yet from the

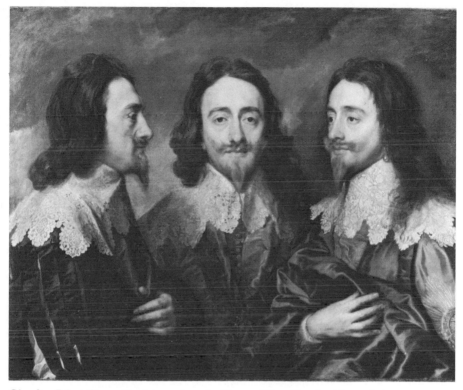

Charles I in Three Positions by Anthony Van Dyck—Copyright reserved to H. M. the Queen, used by permission of the Lord Chamberlain.

first, the King had alienated Henrietta Maria by keeping Buckingham with him constantly. She retaliated by forcing him to communicate through a lady-in-waiting, "else I am sure to be denied," he reported.

Bullying his wife by sending her entire Catholic entourage back to France won instant praise for the King. This was the first sign that Charles might be an improvement over his father. The new King had been heir to the throne for thirteen years, but his subjects hardly knew him. A severe stammer made him unusually shy about speaking in public.

All that the country had been able to count on so far was the new King's pleasing outer appearance. Even as heir to the throne he had impressed England by meeting all requirements for royalty—dignity, majesty, and courtesy. Now at the age of twenty-five, he stood a well-proportioned, 5 feet 2 inches tall. Unlike his roughhewn Scottish father, he was an English gentleman who blushed at the slightest obscenity. And as old John Chamberlain duly reported: "The Court is kept more strait and private than in former time."

But for further hints on future policy, the country would have to watch Charles's public attitudes and actions. For example, would he move to get rid of the hateful, ubiquitous Duke of Buckingham? If the Duke remained, always attached closely to the King's person, then having Charles instead of James on the throne would make little difference. As during James's final three years, the King would have the glory, while Buckingham wielded the power.

All too soon, strong rumors had buzzed through London that Buckingham was in complete charge, that he even controlled the King's personal life. Gossipers claimed that on his own Buckingham had negotiated and actually arranged the marriage of Queen Henrietta Maria and King Charles. And the Duke had made no effort to consult or even inform Parliament. Instead, he had plotted to rush the ceremony before Parliament could meet and forbid the posting of marriage bans.

Commenting on reaction to these stories, John Chamberlain wrote in one of his last letters, dated June 15, 1625, when Charles's first Parliament met: "They begin to mutter about matters of religion, that the King promised them when he was Prince that he would never contract any marriage with conditions derogatory to that we profess." Pointing to the King's giving Buckingham free rein to engage in outright deception,

Queen Henrietta Maria with her Dwarf and his pet monkey Pug,
by Anthony Van Dyck—Courtesy of the National Gallery of Art,
Washington, D.C. Samuel H. Kress Collection.

Chamberlain went straight to the point: "Some spare not to say there that all goes backward since this connivance in religion came in, both in our wealth, valor, honour, and reputation...and it seems that they glance and aim at somebody [Buckingham] for misleading and carrying his rider awry."

In and out of Parliament, those who had cheered the breakdown of negotiations to bring the maturely sensual, flaxen-haired *Catholic* Infanta of Spain to England as Queen, now found themselves forced to accept a gawky *Catholic* princess from France. The choice was questionable, even though when asked if she could stand being married to a Protestant, Henrietta Maria had snapped: "Why not? Was not my father one?" Of course, she neglected to add that her father, Henry IV, more interested in consolidating his power over France than in practicing his religion, had converted to Catholicism.

Buckingham had brought the Queen to England, only to have her turn out to be his chief opposition at court. She despised him, with his tall, dark, and hypnotic beauty, which allowed him to stand between herself and her husband. And she resented his treating her like an ignorant child who needed advice on English social dress and manners.

However, it was not the Queen but Buckingham himself who provided his undoing. "Buckingham's wars," as they were derisively tagged, affected English society top to bottom. The aristocracy, and the middle-class landed gentry and merchants, were taxed or arbitrarily imprisoned. The other 90 percent of English society were subject to abrupt impressment into either military or naval service. Buckingham's management of the war against Spain in 1625—duly declared by the last Parliament of James in 1624—brought unrelieved disaster. Early in 1625, Spain's army routed English soldiers attempting to capture the Palatinate. Later that same year, ignorant naval captains, with sick and starving crews impressed into service against their will, retreated after a week fighting the Spanish at Cádiz. Hundreds of men were lost through mismanagement, incompetence, and disease. Gossipy John Chamberlain wrote:

> Such a rabble of raw and poor rascals have not lightly been seen, and go so unwillingly that they must rather be driven than led. You may guess how base we are grown when one that was pressed hung himself for fear . . . another ran into the Thames and . . . drowned himself, another cut off all his fingers of one hand, and another put out his own eyes with salt.

Charles's first Parliament, meeting in June 1625, took vengeance on Buckingham and his military failure. They specified their opposition to future land war, and refused to vote more than £140,000 for naval warfare, scarcely one-quarter of the sum needed for the slightest degree of success. And they declined to raise taxes to pay off the £700,000 debt facing Charles as he came to the throne.

In the King's opening speech, as reported by Chamberlain, "among other things he told them they had drawn him into a war and they must find the means to maintain it." But in a decided slap at Buckingham, who now commanded the navy in his newest capacity as Lord Admiral, Commons went so far as to vote the tonnage and poundage customs duties for one year only, instead of for the life of the King as had always been done for past monarchs. Lords refused to go along with this break in tradition, and made the King's situation even worse. No tonnage and poundage was voted at all.

Meanwhile, ignoring all past protests, Buckingham carried out a secret promise made to the Queen's brother, Louis XIII of France, in the marriage treaty. He lent ships to the French

King for use against the Huguenots at La Rochelle. John Rushworth, a contemporary, reported that the effect of this news on Parliament was "to exasperate the spirit of that great assembly against the Duke of Buckingham." And without mentioning the Duke, Sir Robert Cotton, a moderate member of Parliament, commented that the King needed the advice of "wise, religious, and worthy servants," instead of "young and simple counsel."

Buckingham took note of all this criticism by appearing personally before Parliament on August 8, 1625. He introduced himself as "a faithful, true hearted Englishman" who would never take action without advice of all the King's ministers in the Privy Council. Further, he promised, he would never show favor to Catholics, and would carry out all existing laws against them.

But he failed to convince Parliament. Both sides took immediate and immovable positions. Following the practice of every previous English monarch, Charles would have no advisers but his own men. And Commons confronted the King with their new ploy, developed and honed in the last years of James's reign. They would vote no money to be spent by ministers whose judgment they distrusted. Boldly they included the name of Buckingham in their denunciation. But the King outwitted them. He forced immediate dissolution of Parliament, even though he faced the war against Spain with no funds.

With no money appropriated, Charles and Buckingham looked everywhere for substitute funds. They cashed Henrietta Maria's large dowry, and at one point thought of selling the crown jewels.

They expected a decisive defeat of Spain, which should mean acquisition of booty on a huge scale. But to their horror and disappointment, Spain roundly repulsed England.

Again the King had to look to Parliament for funds. He

called a new session for February 6, 1626. But first he carefully followed Buckingham's advice on how to stagger the opposition. He appointed six Commons leaders as sheriffs in
their home counties. This meant that such men as the aged
but still powerful Sir Edward Coke, and the thirty-three-year-
old Sir Thomas Wentworth could not leave home to serve
in Parliament.

The King appeared in person and made one of his rare public speeches at the opening session. He warned bluntly: "Parliaments are altogether in my power for the calling, setting,
and dissolution. Therefore, as I find the fruits of them to be
good or evil, they are to continue or not to be."

The Parliament of 1626 saw two men vying for power—
the King's chief minister, Buckingham, versus Sir John Eliot
who took over leadership of Commons. Both thirty-four, and
members of the same wealthy court circles, they had been
close associates in the past. Eliot owed his knighthood, bestowed in 1618, to Buckingham, the royal dispenser of favors.
Until the Parliament of 1625, Eliot had been loyal to Buckingham. But now he led the fight to impeach the Duke, charg-
ing him with "trade and commerce of honour" (the selling of
knighthoods). To force Charles's hand, Eliot announced that
Commons would vote no money until the King abandoned
Buckingham.

In the course of debate Eliot cried out with harsh, fiery
eloquence: "Our honour is ruined, our ships are sunk, our
men perished, not by the sword, not by an enemy, not by
chance, but apparently discerned beforehand out of strong
predictions, by those we trust, by that pretended care and
thrift that makes all our misfortunes."

Charles expressed utter contempt for Parliament's impeachment proceedings by recommending Buckingham for yet another post, Chancellor of Oxford, England's oldest university.

This made no impression on Commons. So the King turned to intimidation of the House of Lords.

Aiming for shock effect, he sent the forty-one-year-old Thomas Howard, Earl of Arundel, a conspicuous opponent of Buckingham, to the Tower on an irrelevant, trumped-up charge —the secret marriage of Arundel's son. This was the same Earl of Arundel who in his earlier days had been a hunting companion and host of King James.

Furious, the House of Lords reacted to the imprisonment of Arundel by voting that no member should be imprisoned during a Parliamentary session unless for treason, felony, or breach of the peace. Thus Charles managed to forge an alliance between Commons and Lords on the issue of Parliamentary immunity—free speech in debate—a fight Commons had been waging alone since the first Parliament of James I. To demonstrate the depth of their defiance, Lords refused further debate on any subject whatever, until the King finally gave in and freed Arundel.

Turning his attention back to Commons, Charles showed that he had learned nothing. He attempted to stop the impeachment proceedings by ordering John Eliot thrown into the Tower for his speech justifying the action against Buckingham. With his usual eloquent tactlessness, Eliot had cried out on the floor of Commons, "In reference to the King he [Buckingham] must be styled the canker in his treasure; in reference to the State, the moth of all goodness."

In case Commons had any lingering doubts about the temperature of his anger, Charles authorized Sir Dudley Carleton, his most discreet and professional spokesman, to warn them: "Gentlemen, move not his Majesty with trenching upon his prerogatives lest you bring him out of love with parliaments."

Despite Carleton's veiled threats, Commons took the same position the Lords had taken on Parliamentary immunity and refused to proceed with any business until Eliot returned to the floor—which he did, after spending eight days in the Tower. Once again the King was forced to save Buckingham by the radical step of dissolving Parliament.

Desperate for money, Charles turned to the counties and boroughs for voluntary payments, only to have them respond that funds could not be raised "save in a parliamentary way." But somehow the King had to pay for England's anti-Catholic crusades abroad. In addition to the continuing war against Spain, he now found himself drawn into war with his wife's brother, the King of France. Louis XIII was set on taking revenge against Charles for failure to give massive support to his effort to suppress the French Huguenots, and for shipping home Henrietta Maria's Catholic attendants so unceremoniously (and thus removing their Catholic influence from the inner circles of the English court).

Forbidden by law and custom to raise taxes without Parliamentary consent, Charles reverted to the Tudor scheme of forced "loans." Money was "exacted, as if, in truth, an act had passed to that purpose," in the words of moderate royal historian Clarendon.

Picking and choosing the precedents he would follow, Charles now found exactly the right one, already used by his father. He too would intimidate the courts by firing his Chief Justice of the King's Bench—in this case, Sir Randolph Crew, who had refused to rule the forced loan legal.

More horrified than frightened at the King's arrogance, Sir Thomas Darnel and four other knights of distinguished old families and enormous influence refused to pay this forced loan. Immediately they found themselves thrown into prison without trial or ceremony. And when they petitioned for a writ of habeas corpus revealing the cause of imprisonment, they were told only that they were imprisoned "by the special command of the King." Furthermore, the now submissive Court of King's Bench ruled that this answer was sufficient in law, and refused to set the prisoners free on bail. The King won his case against the five knights, but the opposition received the favorable publicity.

Meanwhile, Buckingham's wars grew bigger and bloodier. In addition to directing operations against the Catholics of Spain, Buckingham personally led troops to the Isle of Rhé. There, outside La Rochelle, France, he reversed direction and supported the Huguenots against the King of France. But mutiny, poor training, and lack of supplies decimated Buckingham's men.

With Parliament out of session, the King reverted to absolute control over his subjects' lives. He established martial law, impressed into the army or navy any man who could both stand and breathe, and ordered these men billeted in small private homes at ports of embarkation. And when these homes became overcrowded, he ordered the men to be billeted with inhabitants in inland counties.

Taxes affected only those with money to pay them, but impressment, billeting, and martial law brought widespread hardship and distress. Looking back, Sir Walter Earle reported:

> In my county, under colour of placing a soldier, there came twenty in a troop to take sheep. They disturb markets and fairs, rob men on the highway, ravish women, breaking houses in the night and enforcing men to ransom themselves, killing men that have assisted the constable to keep the peace.

Directing heavily armed soldiers to enforce his recently proclaimed martial law, the King managed to terrify everyone— the 2 percent in the upper class and 8 percent in the middle class, both classes well represented in Parliament, as well as the 90 percent who comprised the lower classes and had no actual representation in government. Without any pretense of trial, the King ordered immediate hanging of soldier-criminals. In the future, what or who could stop him from using this same court martial system to hang anyone who got in his way?

In this setting of near-hysteria, the King summoned his third Parliament into session. They convened on March 17, 1628, a date which they and their supporters viewed as two months short of two full years of royal absolutism and chaos. In stark contrast, Charles, living in his own world of art collecting and splendor at court, viewed this same period of rule without Parliament as the only way to preserve intact the power handed down by the Tudors.

Charles decided to release 76 of the men he had imprisoned for failure to pay the forced loan. Of this number, 27 were members of the new Parliament. As actual victims of the King's arbitrary tax and imprisonment policies, they came back determined to fight for a return to the "fundamental laws of Englishmen." In the words of Sir Benjamin Rudyerd: "I shall be very glad to see that good old decrepit law of Magna Charta, which has been kept so long and lain bedridden as it were—I shall be glad to see it walk abroad again, with new vigour and lustre." Sir Benjamin was a prize catch for the Puritans. Once a member in good standing of the royal inner circle—knighted by King James in 1618 and given the highly profitable office of surveyor of the Royal Court of Wards for life—his imprisonment now made him defect to the Puritan side.

In complete agreement with Rudyerd, another member of Parliament and one of Sir Benjamin's companions in prison, Sir Robert Phelips cried out:

I can live, although another without title be put to live with me (viz., billeted on me) nay I can live though I pay excises and impositions more than I do; but to have the liberty which is the soul of my life taken from me by power and to be pent up in a gaol without remedy by law, and to be so adjudged to perish in gaol; O improvident ancestors! O unwise forefathers! to be so curious in providing for the quiet possession of our lands and liberties of Parliament, and to neglect our persons and bodies, and to let them die in prison remediless. If this be law why do we talk of our liberties?

Looking back to this Parliament some thirty-five years later, royal historian Clarendon sounded like the contemporary Puritan opposition: "Could it be imagined that these men would meet again in a free convention of Parliament without a sharp and severe expostulation and inquisition into their own right, and the power that had imposed upon that right?"

But in 1628, Charles continued to stumble and snarl addressing Parliament:

I have called you together, judging a Parliament to be the ancient, speediest, and best way to give such supply as to secure ourselves and save our friends from imminent ruin. Every man must do according to his conscience; wherefore, if you (which God forbid) should not do your duties in contributing what this state at this time needs, I must, in discharge of my conscience, use those other means which God has put into my hands, to save that which the follies of other men may otherwise hazard to lose. Take not this as a threat (for I scorn to threaten any but my equals); but an admonition from him that, both out of nature and duty, has most care of your preservations and prosperities.

Half wheedling, half bullying, he asserted that the behavior of Parliament would determine his willingness to meet with them often, "for be assured that nothing can be more pleasing unto me than to keep a good correspondency with you."

Parliament, however, would not stand for either cajolery or intimidation. Their very existence was at stake. Somehow they had to correct royal arbitrariness for all time.

Near mutiny, the new Parliament sat for three months refusing to provide actual appropriations—until the King agreed to sign the Petition of Right, which they had carefully drawn up and directed at outlawing the harsh abuses of his first three years as King: martial law, billeting, arbitrary taxation, and arbitrary imprisonment. Parliament's mood was radical, its actions conservative. Deliberately, members presented the Petition not as new legislation, but as a reaffirmation of ancient rights, going all the way back to the Magna Carta of 1215.*

For a whole week the King kept putting off action on the Petition of Right. Parliament had offered the King a bribe of five subsidies in return for his signature on the Petition. But Charles found this document a high price to pay. Finally, however, he agreed to sign, telling Parliament: "Now I have done my part; wherefore, if this Parliament has not a happy conclusion, the sin is yours; I am free of it."

---

* As the last major constitutional confrontation between King and Parliament to be witnessed at home in England by many Puritans, the Petition of Right was carried directly to the New World where it contributed both ideas and wording to the first ten amendments to the United States Constitution, known as the Bill of Rights. Imprisonment, or deprivation of life, liberty, or property are in both documents expressly forbidden except by—identical wording—"due process of law." Nor is the England of 1628 or the United States of 1791 ever to be forced to billet soldiers in private homes against the will of the inhabitants. The Petition of Right occupied a place of honor in colonial libraries. But more importantly, eyewitness details of the struggle over its enactments could be passed by word of mouth from one generation to another.

Excited by their greatest success to date, Parliament once again demanded the dismissal of Buckingham. Until the King yielded, they would grant no tonnage and poundage, the ancient royal revenue which, with their inflated notions of power, they were calling "arbitrary taxation" as prohibited by the Petition of Right. They ignored the warning of Sir Benjamin Rudyerd, who, though he still supported the Puritans, pleaded: "Moderation is the virtue of virtues and the wisdom of wisdoms. . . . There can be no total and final loss of liberty but by loss of Parliaments; as long as they last, what we cannot get at one time we may have at another."

The King held one all-powerful trump card, the power to dissolve Parliament. Parliament's power of the purse paled beside this particular royal prerogative. But the King hesitated. He needed money desperately, so decided to recess rather than dissolve Parliament, hoping that time and the implied threat would save the minister he preferred to his wife.

However, support in the streets inflamed Parliament still further. Everywhere members found handbills:

WHO RULES THE KINGDOM?
The King
WHO RULES THE KING?
The Duke
WHO THE DUKE?
The Devil
LET THE DEVIL LOOK TO IT.

The Devil to some was the Duke's physician and astrologer, Dr. Lambe. Leaving the theater one evening the doctor was greeted by cries of "The Duke's Devil! The Duke's Devil!" The mob followed, pelting him with rocks, mud, anything throwable. Then they beat him to death.

Unrepentant, they ran through the streets shouting:

Let Charles and George do what they can
The Duke shall die like Dr. Lambe.

("George" was the crowd's way of demoting the Duke of Buckingham to common status, using his given name George Villiers.)

Shortly after Dr. Lambe's murder, thirty-three-year-old John Felton stabbed Buckingham with a tenpenny dagger. "The villain has killed me," the Duke murmured, pulled out the knife, and keeled over. Felton was caught, hanged, and immediately achieved great following as a folk hero.

In anger and grief at the assassination of Buckingham, the King, acting through Speaker John Finch of the House of Commons, ordered Parliament to remain adjourned. But Parliament was full of angry men: Sir John Eliot who tried twice to have Buckingham removed from office and convicted of crime against England, only to find himself imprisoned by the King and released through the insistence of Parliament; John Rolle who had had his property taken away for refusal to pay taxes; Oliver Cromwell, gentleman farmer, lawyer, and Puritan, who appeared for the first time in Commons as the scarcely noticed new member for Huntingdon; and the King's strongest opponent in the House of Lords and most skillful tactician among Puritan leaders, William Fiennes, who had become the First Viscount Saye and Sele on the death of his father in 1613.

Parliament locked all doors and passed resolutions against granting tonnage and poundage for the life of the King, and against the King's religious policy. The King was using the Church to bolster his claims of royal absolutism much too insistently for Puritan minds. He had gone so far as to call the

Established Church "the chiefest support of royal authority," and throughout his reign he acted on his belief that "people are governed by the pulpit more than the sword in time of peace." Thus, Parliament now specifically defined as a traitor to England—"a capital enemy to this Kingdom and Commonwealth"—anybody supporting the High Church or royal power to levy and collect tonnage and poundage without Parliamentary consent.

The Puritan majority in Parliament also decided to stand their ground on the issue of forced royal adjournment. According to ancient custom, Parliament could continue its session only as long as the Speaker remained in his chair. Therefore, acting for all members of Parliament, strong, young Denzil Holles pushed the courtly but trembling speaker John Finch back into his seat screaming: "God's wounds. You shall sit till we please to rise."

Parliament won a momentary victory, wresting from the King the right to vote its own adjournment on March 2, 1629. But Charles was not finished fighting. He ordered the Royal Guard to break down the doors of Parliament and carry off to the Tower nine offending Puritan leaders. Denzil Holles, one of those ordered under immediate arrest, got away, but not Sir John Eliot, the leader whom the King blamed for Buckingham's death and referred to as "an outlawed man, desperate in mind and fortune." Eliot literally rotted to death within three years, imprisoned in the Tower and heavily guarded.

One week after its momentary victory on adjournment, Parliament had to watch helplessly as the King ordered its final dissolution. He acted according to strict protocol, through the Speaker, who was after all the personal agent of the Crown.

Again the King was master of the situation, and even Parliament's great achievement, the royal signature on the Petition of Right, seemed ready to crumble into invisibility. The King had already ignored the clear proscription of the Petition against arbitrary imprisonment and might very well ignore the rest.

As the Puritans looked around, they saw Catholicism reigning triumphant in Europe with the defeat of the Protestant forces fighting the Spanish-Catholic-Hapsburg alliance. Closer to home they heard stories that Queen Henrietta Maria had begun nagging her husband to abolish all laws suppressing Catholics. And the King's London bishop William Laud, relentlessly silencing Puritan lecturers and driving Puritan preachers underground, seemed ready to return England to papal control.

England was less and less a happy place for Puritans. After the violent adjournment of Parliament and its permanent dissolution by Charles, Puritan lawyer John Winthrop, who was attending the Easter court session in London, wrote to Margaret Tyndal Winthrop, at home in Groton with the children: "My dear wife, these are evil and declining times. . . . I am truly persuaded that God will bring some heavy affliction upon this land, and that speedily."

"Over this Boisterous Billow-Boiling Ocean"

Death almost took John Winthrop twice in 1629. And during his serious illnesses that winter and spring his favorite brother-in-law Thomas Fones, a London apothecary, and his beloved mother, Anne Winthrop, both died. Sadness over final tragedy and gladness over his own miraculous recovery shocked him into abandoning his old life. At the age of forty-one, halfway between youth and second childhood, he became that one in a hundred million who changes the world. "Over this boisterous billow-boiling ocean," in the words of his enthusiastic fellow traveler Edward Johnson, John Winthrop led a company of middle-aged intellectuals and adventurers who declared independence of the mother country even before leaving England.

His grandfather Adam, a well-to-do Suffolk County cloth-maker, had nudged himself and his descendants into the middle-class landed gentry back in 1544 by purchasing Groton Manor, part of the former Catholic monastery of Bury St. Edmunds, from King Henry VIII. His son, also named Adam,

John Winthrop, painting attributed to Charles Osgood—Courtesy of the Harvard University Portrait Collection, Harvard University, Cambridge, Massachusetts.

had trained as a lawyer and crossed the social line from trade to profession, and John Winthrop had added to the family holdings by marrying wisely and well. But inflation, depression in the cloth industry which centered around Suffolk County, and a family of seven children forced him to earn extra money.

Through his influential brother-in-law Emmanuel Downing, he secured a position in His Majesty's court of Wards and Liveries. Winthrop collected huge fees working in this rotting institution, which Henry VIII had founded in 1540 to strengthen his feudal control over landowners. When a landowner died, his widow, or eldest son until he reached twenty-one, became a ward whose estate was turned over to this court. In Stuart practice, this meant extra income for the king by selling the wardship to the highest bidder, or extra favors to be granted by the king to his supporters. For the three court lawyers, the inevitable disputes arising from these arrangements meant ready money. Working in this royal sales office and patronage bureau, Winthrop serviced many clients among prominent families—and was inspired to work even harder at his other London job, attorney to the Parliamentary committee charged with writing legislation.

No evidence has turned up in over 300 years that John Winthrop ever profited dishonestly from his court position. But neither did he ever seek to join his friends in prison. Two of his closest friends, Sir Nathaniel Barnardiston and Sir Francis Barrington, Puritan knights in Parliament resisted the forced loan of 1626 and were thrown into prison. But back in Groton, Winthrop explained in a letter to his twenty-one-year-old son, John Jr., in London: "I wrote not the last week. It was a time of much business and distraction, which took up my mind more than ordinarily." Then he became specific: "Remember my love and service to Sir Francis Barrington, and acquaint him how things have gone in our country," adding conspiratorially, "but you must do it in private."

John Winthrop saw no point to martyrdom. In fact, in June 1627, when restless, sea-loving John Jr. signed on for duty with Buckingham's anti-Catholic campaign on behalf of the French Huguenots at La Rochelle, John Sr. advised: "Be not rash, upon ostentation of valor, to adventure yourself to unnecessary dangers."

John Jr. must have followed his father's advice. He returned unharmed, though two out of three were killed, maimed, or diseased in this disastrously unsuccessful campaign. Still he was determined not to follow John Sr. into the practice of law. The salt smell of the sea in London tickled his nose and teased his brain till one year later he announced his decision to sail to New England under the leadership of forty-year-old John Endecott, a rough-and-ready veteran of the Dutch wars. Prodded by the staunch Puritan minister John White of Dorchester in southwest England, the newly reorganized New England Council was making another attempt at permanent colonization.

Unbelievably, even amid the June 1628, fracas over the King's delay in signing the Petition of Right, the future father of New England wrote to his son: "I am loathe you should think of settling there [New England] as yet, but to be going and coming awhile." And obediently John Jr. wrote back four days later: "For my voyage to New England I do not resolve."

Sometime between June 1628 and mid-May 1629, however, John Winthrop Sr. himself decided on overseas colonization. From London he wrote to his wife: "If the Lord sees it will be good for us, he will provide a shelter and a hiding place for us and others."

By early June 1629, vague decision became firm commitment. He wrote to Margaret: "I am still more confirmed in

John Winthrop, the Younger, artist unknown—Courtesy of the Harvard University Portrait Collection, Harvard University, Cambridge, Massachusetts.

that course which I propounded to you" [emigrating to New England]. For the first time he disclosed, "I think my office is gone" [in the Court of Wards and Liveries]. Two weeks later he repeated that his office was gone, without explaining whether he was fired because of his Puritanism or whether he had simply quit to prepare for his colonizing venture. In any case, just three days later he wrote to Margaret: "Where we shall spend the rest of our short time I know not. My comfort is that you are willing to be my companion in what place or condition severe, in weale or in woe."

The following month of July found John Winthrop and his Puritan friends poring over a charter for trade. Charles I had granted the charter four months earlier on March 4, 1629—two days after the violent adjournment of the King's third and last Parliament, and six days before its final dissolution.

Somehow several Puritans or Puritan sympathizers still in high places lumped together all their decade-long political experience into securing this royal grant to the "Governor and Council of the Massachusetts Bay in New England." They hid the details of their activities so well that their exact maneuvers remain a mystery today. But at least one small hint of chicanery came from Matthew Cradock, who was appointed governor of the new company by the King and who was one of its wealthiest contributors. In a complaint sounding suspiciously like a boast, Cradock remarked that the Puritans had obtained this charter "from his Majesty's especial grace, with great cost, favor of personages of note, and much labor."

The official reason for the new charter was to correct sometimes overlapping and legally messy grants of land. Thus the Massachusetts Bay charter was carefully specific in its grant of land, and in the right to self-government—the right to "have and enjoy all liberties and immunities of free and natural sub-

jects as if they . . . were born within the realm of England."
However, amid all this preciseness there existed a yawning
cavity. Whether through brilliant maneuvering on the part of
the Puritans or exhausted indifference on the part of the King,
the Charter had omitted a key clause—the usual requirement
of London as the place of meeting for the Company board of
directors. And this happy accident would soon spawn the
strongest self-government anywhere in the seventeenth-century world.

Some unspecified time after issuance of the charter, a group
of Puritans, all revolving around the Earl of Lincoln by ties of
blood or marriage, descended on his estate at Tattershall, near
Sempringham and Boston on England's east coast. Leading
Puritan peer Theophilus Fiennes-Clinton, the fourth Earl of
Lincoln, was married to Bridget Fiennes, daughter of the Viscount Saye and Sele of an ancient and aristocratic family. The
Earl's daughter Lady Susan became the wife of John Humfrey, who had already worked on New England colonization
with the Reverend John White and the Dorchester Adventurers. In his turn, John Humfrey shared his enthusiasm and
experience with Isaac Johnson, who owned land in three counties and was married to Lady Arbella, another of Lincoln's sis-
ters. Lincoln's steward, a distant relative who managed his
properties, was Thomas Dudley, who took great pride in his
method of paying off the Earl's debts by raising tenants'
rents.

Not having the proper family or marital connections for immediate acceptance into the inner circle at Tattershall, John
Winthrop found another way to involve himself in the
planned colonization. While the Tattershall group busied itself sealing the charter with money, Winthrop wrote and circulated a pamphlet with a title as long as it was accurate: "Reasons to Be Considered for Justifying the Undertakers of the

Intended Plantation in New England, and for Encouraging Such Whose Hearts God Shall Move to Join with Them in It." It made for titillating propaganda as it revealed the inner thoughts of a propertied Puritan who in middle age was ready to throw over his settled life for resettlement in a distant, unfamiliar, and wildly primitive land.

An oversupply of people and an undersupply of land, he insists, has made man worthless in England: "This land grows weary of her inhabitants, and man . . . who is the most precious of all creatures, is here more vile and base than the earth we tread upon, and of less price among us than a horse or a sheep." Then he appeals to land hunger, comparing crowded England with empty America: "The whole earth is the Lord's garden, and he has given it to the sons of men . . . that man might enjoy the fruits of the earth, and God might have his due glory from the creature. Why then should we stand striving here for places of habitation, many men spending as much labor and cost to recover or keep sometimes an acre or two of land as would procure them many and as good or better in another country, and in the meantime suffer a whole continent as fruitful and convenient for the use of man to lie waste without any improvement."

On the practical side, referring to objections that the New World belongs to the Indians, he answers like a true seventeenth-century English gentleman: "That which lies common and has never been replenished or subdued, is free to any that possess or improve it, for God has given to the sons of men a double right to the earth, a natural right and a civil right." Only land used and cultivated "by their own industry" belongs to men by civil right, he contends. "As for the natives in New England, they enclose no land, neither have any settled habitation, nor any tame cattle to improve the land by, and so have no other but a natural right to those countries. So as if we leave them sufficient for their use, we may lawfully take the rest, there being more than enough for them and us."

After recounting all the benefits to be visited upon the Indians from the English settlement, he adds matter-of-factly that there are few Indians left there anyway since "God has consumed the natives with a great plague."

His conscience clear on the problem of Indians, he faces the question of deserting England at a time of impending disaster: "The departing of a good people from a country does not cause a judgment but foreshadows it, which may occasion such as remain to turn from their evil ways, that they may prevent it, or to take some other course that they may escape it." The examples of Protestants in the German Palatinate and in French La Rochelle, who waited until the end of "their former liberty," he cites as "the woeful spectacle of their ruin," which should "teach us more wisdom to avoid the plague when it is foreseen and not to tarry as they did till it overtakes us."

Quite aware of the series of catastrophes in the colony of Virginia, he ascribes these to "their own sloth." And besides, he points out, failure in Virginia may yet turn to "good use." They demonstrated "great and fundamental errors to be avoided." With a bow in the direction of religion, he lists the first of these errors: "Their main end was carnal not religious." Then he elaborates two more causes of failure: "They used unfit instruments, a multitude of rude and misgoverned persons, the very scum of the land," and above all, "They did not establish a right form of government."

This widely circulated tract came into the hands of his old friend Robert Ryece, Suffolk scholar on ancient civilizations who had worked closely with Winthrop in drafting legislation for Parliament in 1624. Point by point, Ryece disputed Winthrop's arguments.

But John Winthrop no longer saw two sides. He had reviewed every argument too carefully to be turned back. So he responded very formally to his old friend, referring to himself in the third person or by the initials J. W. Titling his answer "Particular Considerations in the case of J. W.," he stated with neither conceit nor modesty: "It has come to that issue as (in all probability) the welfare of the plantation depends upon his going, for divers of the chief undertakers (upon whom the rest depend) will not go without him." Referring to his private finances, he explained:

> Though his means be sufficient for a comfortable subsistence in a private condition here, yet the one half of them being disposed to his three elder sons, who are now of age, he cannot live in the same place and calling with that which remains; his charge being still as great as before, when his means were double.

Saving his blockbuster for last, he concluded: "If he should refuse this opportunity, that talent which God hath bestowed upon him for public service, were like to be buried." (Winthrop shared with all Puritans the idea of a "calling," by which God—as revealed through each man's own reason—directed every human being to use to the full his divinely bestowed talents and opportunities.) Winthrop had long wanted to do more than operate around the fringes of politics. Before the final dissolution of Charles's Parliament he had strongly hinted at running himself. With Parliamentary service now out of the question, he had to find a personal alternative.

Ryece tried one last time, however, letting loose a stream of harsh arguments: "The Church and Commonwealth here at home have more need of your best ability in these dangerous times than any remote plantation." Pointing to Winthrop's intellectuality, he reminded him sharply: "How hard will it be for one brought up among books and learned men, to live in a barbarous place, where is no learning and less civility."

But Ryece was too late. By July 1629, Isaac Johnson had sent a letter to Emmanuel Downing and John Winthrop, his brother-in-law, to meet with the Puritan inner circle at Tattershall. Always looking for the good omen, Winthrop found his decision reinforced as he rode horse with his brother-in-law to Lincolnshire, over the swampy East Anglian terrain. His horse fell under him in a bog, leaving him in water up to his waist. When he emerged half-soaked, but completely unhurt, he knew that the Lord would "preserve me from further danger."

Winthrop spent two full weeks at Tattershall, closeted with leading Puritans, mostly from East Anglia* and London. These men had read every word of the Massachusetts Bay Charter of March 1629. Now they were set on beginning their new relationship 3,000 miles across the sea by declaring independence from England.

Back in London at the end of July, they met at the home of Deputy Governor Thomas Goffe, a politically moderate Puritan. On Tuesday, July 28, 1629, Matthew Cradock, governor of the company, read his own revolutionary proposal for the group's consideration: "That for the advancement of the plantation, the inducing and encouraging persons of worth and quality to transplant themselves and families thither, and for other weighty reasons therein contained, to transfer the government of the plantation to those that shall inhabit there, and not to continue the same in subordination to the Company

* The still-used name of the medieval kingdom occupying the land between the Wash and the Thames: the counties of Norfolk, Suffolk, Essex, and part of Lincoln.

here, as it now is." In other words, those who colonized New England would set up their own government there. The new colonists would separate themselves both physically and formally from the parent trading company, which had originally received the royal charter.

If successful, Cradock's proposal could set a radical pattern for colonization. But if the King reconsidered or rewrote the charter, "persons of worth and quality" might find no reason to uproot themselves for life in the untried wilderness. Impatiently, some called for instant action, while others demanded postponement of further discussion to the August meeting of the General Court (seventeenth-century words for "general meeting"). Without question, some cautious members argued, the proposal was contrary to the original idea of setting up a trading company, which would reimburse London investors. Cradock's proposal struck them as illegal, or unprofitable—or probably, both.

In preparation for the August meeting, two committees were set up, one to argue *pro*, the other *con*. And though Company Governor Cradock suggested no formal conspiracy, he warned members "to carry the business secretly so that the same be not divulged."

The date set for the meeting was August 29, 1629. But without waiting for the formal vote of the General Court, twelve men signed mutual pledges three days before at Cambridge. They agreed to emigrate with their families to New England for permanent residence, provided that the charter and the government it established could be transferred completely and legally to their new settlement. The key words of this first declaration of independence were: "Provided always, that, before the last of September next, the whole government, together with the patent for the said plantation, be first legally transferred and established to remain with us and others which shall inhabit upon the said plantation."

When the regular August meeting of the General Court convened, a mere 27 members out of a membership of 125 attended. Seven signers of the Cambridge Agreement—not including John Winthrop for some unknown reason—were present to argue in favor of removal of the charter. And they won the vote, maybe because only those favorable to the charter removal bothered to come. The others were probably more interested in finding safe investments at home than in setting up a New World utopia.

Three weeks later John Winthrop attended his first meeting of the General Court. He had succeeded in winning the support of his two closest confidants: his wife Margaret—she had once worried about his traveling 10 miles down the Thames River to London during the winter, but now resigned herself to an ocean crossing for the entire family—and his oldest son, John Jr. Returning from a fourteen-month sea voyage to the Near East, John Jr. had written to his father just five days before the signing of the Cambridge Agreement: "For the business of New England I can say no other thing, but that I believe confidently that the whole disposition thereof is of the Lord."

Recruitment began for the new colony, and a balladeer sang:

> Stay not amongst the wicked
> Lest that with them you perish
> But let us to New England go
> And the pagan people cherish.

Still the King paid no attention to the goings-on of the Massachusetts Bay Company. Exultantly, Roger Clap, who cast aside his life as English servant for God and adventure in

Massachusetts Bay, explained in his *Memoirs:* "Was it not a wondrous good Hand of God to incline the Heart of our King so freely to grant [the patent of a tract of Land], with all the Privileges which the Patent expresseth?"

Others have since found other explanations for the King's attitude—or at least reasonably educated conjectures. Preparing to rule by himself without even a pretense of Parliamentary advice or consent, the King may have welcomed the departure of Puritan troublemakers. Or he may have been ignorant of the charter's exact wording, or may not have recognized its significance. Or he may have been spending his royal time getting to know his Queen Henrietta Maria, now that Buckingham no longer stood between husband and wife, or negotiating to have the great Flemish painters Anthony Van Dyck and Peter Paul Rubens come to artistically barren England for a prolonged stay and to receive knighthoods.

Whatever the King's reasons, the next development within the Massachusetts Bay Company came out of the blue—the historians' way of saying that no written document, gossip, or even insinuation exists to explain it. At its October 1629 meeting the company chose John Winthrop as its governor. Reminiscing some five years later, John Winthrop acknowledged: "I was first chosen to be Governor without my seeking or expectation, there being divers other gentlemen, who, for their abilities everyway, were far more fit."

John Winthrop had to defeat some impressive competition to win the governorship: Richard Saltonstall, first to sign the Cambridge Agreement, a wealthy London merchant, and nephew and heir of the Lord Mayor of London; Isaac Johnson, wealthiest of the emigrants and an early member of the Puritan inner circle through his brother-in-law the Earl of Lincoln; and longtime widower John Humfrey, treasurer of the old Dorchester Adventurers, part of the predecessor company of Massachusetts Bay, who in the midst of the meetings about the charter had married into the inner circle through his second wife, Lady Sarah Fiennes.

John Winthrop himself had attended his first meeting of the company only the previous month, and though he had spent at least two weeks in the company of the Lincolnshire Puritans late in July, he had no kinship with any of the most influential members. He was, however, known to all through his extensive travels for the Court of Wards and Liveries. And he seemed perfect for the role of governor—conscientious, even-tempered, and distinguished-looking. Whatever the reason, at the October 20, 1629, meeting of the General Court, in the words of the official records, "having received of extraordinary great commendations of Mr. John Winthrop, both for his integrity and sufficiency, as being one every [way] well fitted and accomplished for the place of Governor," the company elected John Winthrop governor for the colony's make-or-break first year.

With incredible speed under Winthrop's direction, ships were hired, supplies furnished, practice of professions suspended, and businesses sold out—all in preparation for the sailing of seventeen ships holding about a thousand colonists and setting out from the end of March 1630. Every detail was carefully planned, even to the choice of four different ports to avoid confusion and overcrowding—Bristol in the west, Plymouth in the southeast, Southampton in the south, and London.

Profiting from the miserable, often fatal, experience of the Pilgrims who had set sail late in the fall only to be tossed unmercifully by an inhospitable winter sea, the Puritans left at the very beginning of the spring season. The lead ship *Arbella*, carrying John Winthrop, arrived just seventy-five days later at four o'clock in the morning, June 12, 1630. It anchored off what is today Massachusetts's North Shore where, Winthrop wrote in the journal he began the day of departure: "There was so pleasant a sweet air as did much refresh us, and there came a smell off the shore like the smell of a garden."

Before embarking from England, the Puritans had read all the literature on overseas exploration, from the first English geographer Richard Hakluyt, to adventurer and map-maker John Smith, to the most recent voyager Reverend Francis Higginson. *A True Relation of the Last Voyage to New England* written by Higginson, described the voyage of two to three hundred colonists, sailing in five ships, led by John Endecott of the Dorchester Company a little more than a year before— and set many a mind at rest about the sea voyage.

Deliberately the Puritans chose the area around Massachusetts Bay as their destination. (John Smith had named the area for the Indian tribe *Mass-adchu-seuk*, meaning "big hill people" and referring to the Blue Hills on the edge of Boston. Smith had pluralized the name to refer to the tribe and simplified it for English tongues and ears—Massachusets. Some later arrival added an extra "t" probably for balance.) Virginia was too Anglican for Puritan purposes and had recently had its charter revoked by the King. The areas between New England and Virginia were more or less controlled by the Dutch, with the French hovering threateningly to the north and west. And the Caribbean was still the domain of the Spanish. On the other hand, the Plymouth Colony showed signs of slow but steady progress after a bad start, and Winthrop's own information that disease had emptied the area of Indians made Massachusetts Bay a logical choice.*

Among the signatories of the Cambridge Agreement who

---

* Puritans who wanted to abandon England but not for the New World settled in Holland's major cities—Amsterdam, Delft, and Rotterdam in the years 1629–1642. Possibly they lacked the necessary

accompanied John Winthrop to New England as assistants of the company were two of his rivals for governor, Richard Saltonstall and Isaac Johnson. (Johnson was the wealthiest of the emigrants, and perhaps to insure his continued enthusiasm and financial support, the name of the lead ship had been changed from *The Eagle* to *Arbella*, in honor of his wife, also a passenger on board.) Winthrop's other fellow signatories and Assistants—all bursting with wealth, intelligence, and healthy middle age—were Thomas Dudley, Increase Nowell, William Pinchon, Thomas Sharpe, and William Vassall. John Humfrey, another candidate for governor who had been scheduled to sail, changed his mind at the very last minute and had to be replaced as Deputy Governor by Thomas Dudley, at fifty-four the oldest of the group (he had been old enough to cheer the English defeat of the Spanish Armada back in 1588). John Humfrey eventually followed with his wife, so that in the end nine who had signed the Cambridge Agreement went to New England, while three others decided to remain in England permanently.

Margaret Winthrop had also remained behind—temporarily, because of pregnancy. Her husband left her in the care of John Jr., who was supervising the sale and disposal of Groton Manor. On board the *Arbella*, John Winthrop wrote tenderly to his wife that preparations for the journey had exhausted him, but he now looked forward to some leisure, during which "I shall not avoid remembrance of thee, nor the grief for thy absence. . . . I hope the course we have agreed upon will be some ease to us both. Mondays and Fridays, at five of the clock at night, we shall meet in spirit till we meet in person."

---

stamina or sense of adventure. Or possibly they had no desire to seize the reins of self-government, increasingly feasible in New England.

Margaret Winthrop may have kept the spiritual rendez-vous faithfully. Her husband had to concentrate almost every waking thought on transforming a hostile wilderness into home for a thousand stubborn individualists.

"Chosen by Papers"

"Their too large commendations of the country" led the Company to New England, Deputy Governor Thomas Dudley complained in a disaster-filled letter March 12, 1631. He and his companions saw "the colony in a sad and unexpected condition," many dead from disease or starvation, he wrote to the Countess of Lincoln, wife of his former employer at Tattershall, nine months after his arrival in America. And they were "glad to be rid of" about a hundred ("some think many more") who returned home on the same ships that had brought them, "partly out of dislike for our government, which restrained and punished their excesses and partly through fear of famine (not seeing other means than by their labor to feed themselves)."

Sheer survival became the problem for the Puritans from the time they left England—despite all their reading, careful organization, and large stock of supplies. Looking back on that first year, an early settler, William Wood, mourned: "Their bodies were corrupted with sea-diet, which was naught, their beef and pork being tainted, their butter and cheese corrupted, their fish rotten, and voyage long, by reason of cross winds, so that winter approaching before they could get warm houses, and the searching sharpness of that purer climate, creeping in at the crannies of their crazed bodies, caused death and sickness." Three such deaths struck close to John Winthrop. The day after his safe landing at Salem, twenty-two-year-old Henry Winthrop suffered an attack of cramps and drowned in a small creek. One month later the fragile Lady Arbella died, unable to survive the change "from a paradise of plenty and pleasure which she enjoyed in the family of a noble earldom to a wilderness of wants." And shortly afterward, her husband Isaac Johnson, "the chiefest man of estate in the land," grieved himself to death. Edward Johnson (no relation) penned some verse in his memory, a rare feat among Puritans, generally too busy struggling to survive and to establish a stable government to have time for irrelevant creativity:

> Oh, people, why doth Christ deny this world's life to
> lengthen?
> Christ only trust, Johnson's turned dust, and yet he's
> crowned and strengthened.

During the first year, 200 had died, mostly from fever or scurvy. Dr. Samuel Fuller, a settler sent from the older Plymouth Colony to give all possible help, wrote to his own Governor William Bradford when a scurvy epidemic around Massachusetts Bay broke out: "I here but lose time and long to be at home. I can do them no good for I want drugs and things fitting to work with."

Despite enveloping tragedy, John Winthrop glossed his letters to Margaret with optimism. He described but refused to complain about "coarse" food: "I may truly say I desire no better." He advised his wife to ignore "anything that you shall hear from hence, for I see no reason to repent of coming hither," even though "Satan bends his forces against us, and stirs up his instruments to all kind of mischief."

Salem, where the newcomers first settled took its name from the Hebrew *shalom*—"peace." But Winthrop and company found themselves constantly threatened by hostile intruders—the French, the Spanish, and wolves who ate their cattle and pigs. They decided to look for another area where God could more easily help them to help themselves.

Advance parties went out to explore up and down the coast, in and around myriad islands, inlets, and rivers. Finally the company decided on Charlestown as their seat of government. The area, ironically named for the very King they were fleeing, was a peninsula on the Bay, easier to fortify, and protected against the wind by surrounding islands.

Most of the company followed, sailing the 15 miles from Salem in tiny pinnaces, or hacking their way overland through dense woods. Grateful at last to find their home away from home, they pitched their tents, wigwams, and the rickety temporary shelters they euphemistically called "cottages."

But they had started out from land-hungry England as a group of nonconforming individualists. And so, immediately, several wandered off to settle in the empty wilderness surrounding Charlestown: Dorchester through Roxbury in the south, Newtowne (later renamed Cambridge) and Watertown in the west, and Saugus and Medford in the north. Deputy Governor Dudley explained to the Countess of Lincoln: "Salem where we landed pleased us not. . . . Our dispersion troubled some of us, but help it we could not, wanting ability to remove to any place fit to build a town upon, and the time too short to deliberate longer lest the winter should surprise us before we had builded our houses."

As soon as they were somewhat settled, Governor Winthrop summoned the deputy governor and assistants of the company to the first court (meeting) on New World soil, Monday, August 23, 1630. They met "in the open air under a tree," Roger Clap later recalled. As a twenty-two-year-old indentured servant, he had witnessed the meeting, probably from a respectful distance.

This first meeting dealt with creature comforts and practical needs, such as additional housing, food supplies, town boundaries, encouraging trade, and establishing maximum wages to prevent taking advantage of future arrivals. Also, Winthrop, Dudley, and the assistants concerned themselves with providing food and shelter for the ministry, levying taxes, and appointing officers to carry out laws and regulations.

The Bay Colony seemed finally on the way to survival and stability when its members had their first encounter with the very un-English, semitropical heat of Massachusetts in August. Unhappily, they had to pick themselves up from Charlestown, and try setting up their government in Boston, just across the river. The always observant Edward Johnson explained the decision to move, even at the expense of having to dismantle and bring along the frame of the Governor's house, already under construction: "That which added to their present distress [in Charlestown] was the want of fresh water; for although the place did afford plenty, yet for the present they could find but one spring, and that not to be come at but when the tide was down."

To their astonishment the Winthrop group arrived at Boston to find the place already inhabited by a white man. He was thirty-five-year-old William Blackstone, a Cambridge University man. And he had been the only resident for several years. Blackstone allowed the Puritans to use his spring, sold them his

excellent lands, and generally helped them to establish themselves in the area, even though he claimed the whole peninsula for himself "because he was the first that slept upon it,"
as Massachusetts Bay historian Thomas Hutchinson reported
in 1765.

No one has ever figured out how or exactly when Blackstone arrived. But he dropped strong hints as to why he came
—a lifelong disdain for organized society. As soon as the Puritans showed signs of becoming highly organized, he took off
to wild Rhode Island, carrying along his collection of books.
According to Hutchinson, Blackstone informed the Puritans
before his departure that "he came from England because he
did not like the Lords Bishop, but he could not join with them
because he did not like the Lords Brethren."

Fascinated in the overorganized, overcrowded twentieth
century by the man who prized privacy and nature, poet Conrad Aiken mused: *

WILLIAM BLACKSTONE (*Died 1675*)
Where now he roves, by wood or swamp whatever,
the always restless, always moving on,
his books burned, and his own book lost forever,
under the cold stars of New England, gone,

scholar who loved, and therefor left, the most,
secret and solitary, no Indian-giver,
who to his own cost played the generous host
and asked adventurers across his river.

. . . .

* From *Collected Poems* by Conrad Aiken. Copyright © 1953, 1970
by Conrad Aiken. Reprinted by permission of Oxford University
Press, Inc.

the common field he found and kept aright,
setting his rose-trees and his fruit trees out:
these, and his books, and truth, all his delight,
and the locked heart of man his only doubt. . . .

After the final and comparatively painless uprooting of the
government from Charlestown to Boston, only eight members
showed up for the first formal meeting of the General Court,
October 16, 1630. Desperate to insure permanence amidst all
the death, distress, and danger, Winthrop and his cohorts decided to correct forever this small turnout of officialdom. They
threw open the meeting to all freemen (adult males who were
not servants), and thereby launched the first American revolution in government.

The Massachusetts Bay Company reinterpreted the actual
words of their trading company charter, and quietly added
some unwritten ones of their own over the next four years. In
the usual cut-and-dried fashion for trading companies, the
original charter had given the company a governor (more or
less equivalent to a twentieth-century chairman of the
board), a council of eighteen assistants (serving the function
of a modern board of directors), and a general court of freemen (investors), all of whom were to meet together four times
a year.

At just this point, the carefully nurtured omission of the requirement that these meetings be held in London boom-
eranged. Most of the assistants had resigned back in England.
And only about eight of the company's original hundred or so
freemen had come to the colony. Failure loomed so large for
the whole venture that John Winthrop and his fellow directors were forced to resort to on-the-spot improvisation. By
broadening the definition of freemen, they gave the company
a government of one hundred sixteen freemen out of a total

population of about a thousand men, women, children, and servants. The number of freemen grew as the population grew. And step by step these freemen won increasing participation in government, until by 1634 they were allowed the right to vote at the annual election for governor, deputy governor, and assistants, and could themselves be elected to these offices.*

In the very beginning, then, New England leaped four radical steps beyond the seventeenth century. First and maybe foremost, they based their action of throwing open that initial general meeting of October 1630 on popular consent: "This was fully assented unto by the general vote of the people," the official record read. Second, the responsibility for voting and for holding office was shared by all who were citizens, thus providing a rein on absolutism. Third, they had served notice that the charter could be changed or reinterpreted whenever circumstances required. And finally, they omitted members of the clergy from all government offices: governor, assistants, and justices of the peace.

In this connection, almost a century and a half later, historian Thomas Hutchinson told the tale of Increase Nowell, one of the original twelve signers of the Cambridge Agreement of 1629. Nowell had been elected an assistant of the company at the same time that John Winthrop was elected Governor. On his arrival in Charlestown, he was elected ruling elder of the Church, but soon resigned this Church position in order to continue to serve on the Court of Assistants. Serving in the Church and having, in Hutchinson's words, "a place in

---

* In contrast, Sir William Petty, founder-member of the Royal Society of English Scientists and pioneer in using statistics, wrote in 1660 that Parliamentary elections "are governed by less than 2,000 active men." The population of England and Wales at that time is estimated at between 3,500,000 and 5,000,000.

the civil order were thought, in that day not well to consist, and therefore he quitted it choosing the place of assistant."

Yet it was still one nation, one religion. Puritans had no quarrel with this seventeenth-century European ideal, provided that the single national religion was "purified" and changed to meet their own exacting standards. (It was for such insistence that their grandfathers had been dubbed "Puritans" in 1564 by Queen Elizabeth's Archbishop of Canterbury, Matthew Parker.) Carrying out his own strong convictions on religious unity, John Winthrop once went to the extreme of changing the name of Hue's Cross—a small place he passed on his way from Boston to Plymouth on a visit to Governor Bradford—to Hue's Folly. Otherwise, he insisted, "such things might hereafter give the Papists occasion to say that their religion was first planted in these parts."

The same thinking motivated a law passed by the General Court in the spring of 1631: "For time to come no man shall be admitted to the freedom of this body politic, but such as are members of some of the churches within the same." A freeman might have no wealth, but he must be one of God's elect, a "Visible Saint." Otherwise, the infant government would be threatened either by local subversives or by those sent over from England by the King and his bishop Laud. The Puritans could at times sound and act as modern as tomorrow. But in this case they were very much children of the seventeenth century, insisting that unity in religion and agreement in politics must exist together or not at all.*

John Winthrop was repeatedly elected Governor in the years, 1630–1634. In his ebullient history, *Wonder-Working Providence of Sion's Saviour in New England,* Edward

---

* The religious requirement for freemanship was finally dropped in 1664.

Johnson exulted: "John Winthrop Esq. was chosen Governour, picked out for the work by the provident hand of the most high and enabled with gifts accordingly." Then Johnson felt it his duty to "remember him in this . . . meter":

> Why leavest thou, John, thy station, in Suffolk, thy own soil,
> Christ will have thee a pillar be, for's people thou must toil;
> He changed thy heart, then take his part, 'gainst prelates
>   proud invading.
> His Kingly throne set up alone, in wilderness their shading.
> · · · · · · · · · · · · · · · · · · ·
> By name and note, with people's vote, their Governour
>   to be.

John Winthrop and company were original doers, but not particularly original thinkers. From their religion they borrowed covenant theory to establish civil government—the same theory already used politically by their friends and fellow countrymen, the neighboring Pilgrims, in their Mayflower Compact. Aboard the *Arbella*, John Winthrop had explained that their very act of boarding ship together for the New World meant that they had agreed to establish a government. And this would be a government based on consent of the governed: "It is by mutual consent through a special overruling providence to seek out a place of cohabitation . . . under a due form of government both civil and ecclesiastical." In addition to being both political and religious, this government would be independent: "Thus stands the cause between God and us; we are entered into covenant with him for this work. We have taken out a commission, the Lord hath given us leave to draw our own articles." (In the twentieth century the United States bases its government on covenant theory as set forth in the Declaration of Independence of 1776—". . . men

. . . are endowed by their Creator with certain unalienable rights. . . . To secure these rights, governments are instituted among men deriving their just powers from the consent of the governed"—and the Constitution of 1787, introduced by a preamble including the words, "We the people of the United States in order to form a more perfect union . . . do ordain and establish this constitution for the United States of America.")

Democracy in Puritan New England was still far off, but class distinctions began crumbling immediately. Even men who had sailed from England as indentured servants could become freemen by working off their indenture. And most importantly, each individual had charge of his own destiny— unless his actions hurt others, at which point controls were instituted for the general good of the community.

For example, John Winthrop explained why what has since been called the "Puritan Ethic," had to include rigorous wage and price control:

> The scarcity of workmen had caused them to raise their wages to an excessive rate, so as a carpenter would have three shillings the day, a laborer two shillings and six-pence, etc.; and accordingly those who had commodities to sell advanced their prices sometimes double to what they cost in England, so as it grew to a general complaint, which the court, taking knowledge of, as also of some further evils, which were sprung out of the excessive rates of wages, they made an order that carpenters, masons, etc. should take but two shillings the day, and laborers but eighteen pence, and that no commodity should be sold at above four pence in the shilling more than it cost for ready money in England.

Further elaborating on the need for stringent regulation,

Governor Winthrop pointed to "the evils which were spring-
ing: 1. Many spent much time idly, etc., because they could
get as much in four days as would keep them a week. 2. They
spent much in tobacco and strong waters, etc., which was a
great waste to the commonwealth, which by reason of so
many foreign commodities expended, could not have subsisted
to this time, but that it was supplied by the cattle and corn,
which were sold to newcomers at very dear rates, viz. corn at
six shillings the bushel, a cow at £20,—yea, some at £24,
some £26—a mare at £35, an ewe goat at £3 or £4; and yet
many cattle were every year brought out of England, and
some from Virginia."

In case anybody escaped regulation by law, John Winthrop
appealed to self-regulating righteousness. He produced an
anecdote, complete with the moral that there is a definite connection between wealth and godliness. He told the story of a
poor man named Mansfield who had come to America. Here,
a wealthy merchant, one Marshall, gave him an outright gift
of £50, and lent him another £100. But, Winthrop sermon-
ized in his journal: The once poor "Mansfield grew suddenly
rich, and then lost his godliness, and his wealth soon after."

With English prices and New England government, Massachusetts Bay was beginning to look like utopia—despite or
maybe because of the government's firm notice that part of its
responsibility was to prevent idleness, drunkenness, swearing,
lying, or disobedience. The government also ruled against excesses in dress, though the magistrates allowed the Puritans to
wear the bright colors they liked so much. Anyone who objected to regulation need not come, and those already present
were free to leave. With people pouring in on each newly arrived ship from England, there was no need for Massachusetts
to lower its admission requirements. By 1633, there were between three and four thousand apparently acceptable people,

scattered in sixteen towns as far distant as Ipswich, thirty miles from Boston, the capital.

But utopia was still a rough-and-ready frontier, and as such was bound to include insolent individualists with no respect for authority. There was, for instance, John Stone, captain of a small pinnace, who when called to court for disturbing the peace, addressed Justice Roger Ludlow as "just ass." The jury hearing his case may inwardly have enjoyed this bit of comic relief, but they fined him £100 and ordered him banished from the colony, to reenter only on pain of death. They dismissed the main charge because of lack of sufficient evidence.

In his journal, Governor Winthrop reported some crimes and punishments administered by the Court of Assistants, which had judicial as well as legislative authority for maintaining law and order. At the court of June 1631, a servant Philip Ratcliff was convicted "of most foul, scandalous invectives against our church and government, and was censured to be whipped, lose his ears and be banished from the plantation, which was presently executed." "At the same court," Winthrop noted, "one Henry Linne was whipped and banished for writing letters into England full of slander against our government and orders of our churches."

Another major responsibility for the assistants was preventing maltreatment of the Indian natives. Anybody disobeying the new government's proclaimed respect for property and morality suffered immediate punishment. This included rich men, poor servants, and occasionally Indians themselves (when their behavior threatened the stability of the "heaven-sent" Puritan settlement). Josias Plaistowe and his servants were convicted of stealing four baskets of corn from the natives. Plaistowe was required to return eight baskets to Chickatabot, chief of the local Massachusetts Indians, fined five pounds, and "degraded from the title of a gentleman"—

i.e., to be addressed in the future as Josias, no longer entitled to be called "Mr." Plaistowe. At the same time his servants were whipped.

Thomas Morton, a longtime troublemaker who had taught the Indians the use of guns, came before the court accused of shooting at, though not hurting, a group of Indians who refused to give him their canoe. His punishment was to

> be set into the bilboes, and after to be sent prisoner into England . . .: that all his goods shall be seized upon to defray the charge of his transportation, payment of his debts, and to give satisfaction to the Indians for a canoe he unjustly took from them; and that his house, after the goods are taken out, shall be burnt down to the ground in the sight of the Indians, for their satisfaction, for many wrongs he hath done them from time to time.

On another occasion the sachem Chickatabot, who had himself shot one of Richard Saltonstall's swine, was fined one beaver skin. However, punishment of the Indians in the early years was rare. More prevalent was the attitude expressed in 1632: "The more love and respect you show to the sagamores and sachems [the Puritans used both words to designate Indian chiefs] the more love and fear shall you gain from the common natives."

During the very months when the court was preoccupied with setting standards of lawful and social behavior, and introducing the Indians to English jurisprudence, a small event reminded New Englanders of the precariousness of their position. Winthrop noted in his journal: "Mr. Ludlow, in digging the foundation on his house at Dorchester, found two pieces of French money: one was coined in 1596. They were above a foot within the firm ground." Shortly afterward, the gov-

Richard Saltonstall, Sr. (1586–1661)—Used by permission of the
Peabody Museum of Salem, Massachusetts.

ernor reported: "The French came in a pinnace to Penobscot, and rifled a trucking house belonging to Plymouth, carrying thence three hundred weight of beaver and other goods. They took also one Dixy Bull and his shallop and goods."

Having the French preying at will on their property was frightening. So was the threat of a full-scale invasion, which made the government decide to fortify Newtowne, where they had recently built houses for the Governor and Deputy Governor in hopes of reuniting the scattered communities. Whether on purpose or by mistake, they did not abandon the planned fortifications with the disappointment of these hopes and the subsequent return to Boston as the capital town.

In an early display of "no taxation without representation" Watertown in February 1632 protested against the levying of taxes for what they apparently considered a local project. Newtowne might or might not become the capital of their commonwealth, but it was not their own town. They refused to "pay moneys of that sort, for fear of bringing themselves and posterity into bondage."

The Watertown protesters were successful, John Winthrop noted in his journal. Henceforth, each town would appoint two representatives "to advise with the governor and assistants about the raising of a public stock so as what they should agree upon should bind all." Again giving the future something to work with, New England had set up a forerunner of the federal system of government. Local governments would control local affairs, and they would also be represented in the general colonial government. Town Meetings,* attended by all resident freemen, began convening quarterly,

---

* Transplanted to New England, the Town Meeting used an old name to veer off in a new direction. The idea came from the East Anglian Town Meeting, originally a parish assembly, established with the blessing of the king to carry out royal edicts or proclamations.

with responsibility for public health (which included forced cleanliness of the butchery or leather works), police protection, roads, education, and—far afield from the so-called Puritan Ethic—an adequate supply of food, clothing, and shelter for the poor. Routine administration was left to a small group of selectmen—men selected from the general electorate and supervised by the Town Meeting—who met on a monthly basis.

However, the freemen were still unhappy. They were represented in the General Court, but it was the towns and not they themselves who chose the deputies. They fought this for two more years. In 1634, they finally won the right to elect their own deputies to act for them in the General Court—making laws, distributing land, imposing taxes, and dealing with "all other affairs of the commonwealth wherein the freemen have to do."

At last the freemen were satisfied. They would continue to be present in person at the annual spring election meeting of the General Court. In addition, they would send their own elected town deputies to the other three quarterly meetings of the General Court. All this should keep the magistrates from going off on a deluge of arbitrariness, they reasoned, because they would be surrounded by popular representatives able to restrain them. In the seventeenth century, then, the freemen of Massachusetts Bay had defined a basic human right, which the twenty-first century may yet grant universally—the right to representative government based on the consent of the governed.

John Winthrop had been governor during all the turmoil accompanying these four years of radical change. If he had expected peace and quiet, or even gratitude, he found himself instead fending off a barrage of public complaints from his Deputy Governor, Thomas Dudley. Senior in age by thirteen years, but inferior in education, wealth, and public experience, Dudley coveted the office of governor.

Each man had his followers in the colony. Winthrop's supporters defended their governor for treating each offense charitably on its merits, and always bearing in mind the unsettled state of the community. The Dudley faction objected that too much leniency would lead to fatal disaster.

"By what authority had the Governor given license to Ratcliff and Grey (being banished men) to stay within our limits," Winthrop impersonally recorded Dudley as demanding.

"The Governor answered," Winthrop quoted himself as saying, "he did it by that authority, which was granted him in court, viz., that upon any sentence in criminal causes, the Governor might, upon cause, stay the execution till the next court. Now the cause was that being in the winter, they must otherwise have perished."

"Why were the fines not levied," Dudley persisted.

"The Governor answered, it belonged to the secretary and not to him. He never refused to sign any that were brought to him. Nay, he had called upon the secretary for it. Yet he confessed, that it was his judgment that it were not fit, in the infancy of a commonwealth to be too strict in levying fines, though severe in other punishments."

Winthrop reported the dispute so routinely and impersonally that the first editor of his journal, James Savage, in the early nineteenth century, must have felt obliged to come to his aid with a note: "Winthrop and Dudley were men differently constituted. While Winthrop was mild, disposed to lenience, and always a seeker of peace, Dudley was intolerant, uncompromising, of quick temper, and disposed to ride roughshod."

After serving four consecutive terms as governor, Winthrop could have made good use of this flattering comparison. The two years following the Watertown protest of 1632 had brought significant participation in government to the freemen, only to make them eager to test the new system—by throwing John Winthrop out of office. They reduced him to the rank of assistant, and elected his arch rival Thomas Dudley as governor. Either Massachusetts freemen were thinking in politically sophisticated terms of rotation in office as a means to prevent tyranny—or else the Dudley faction, conducting the first successful political campaign against an incumbent, convinced them that they had had enough of Winthrop for a while.

In any case, this precedent-setting election of 1634, demonstrated strong resistance by the citizenry to a closer tie between Church and State, even though there was as yet no formal separation of Church and State. They went so far as to ignore the election sermon of their learned and beloved forty-nine-year-old minister John Cotton who had arrived from Boston, England, the previous year, after a narrow escape from the authorities there. (Some said that the New England Puritans had named their capital city Boston in his honor and in hopes of enticing him to New England sooner.) John Winthrop reported in his journal: "Master Cotton preached and delivered this doctrine that a magistrate ought not to be turned into the condition of a private man without just cause, and to be publicly convict, no more than the magistrates may not turn a private man out of his freehold, etc."

Then Winthrop concluded succinctly: "The court chose a new governor, viz., Thomas Dudley Esq. the former deputy, and Mr. Ludlow was chosen deputy. . . . The court was kept in the meeting-house at Boston, and the new governor and the assistants were together entertained at the house of the old governor, as before." In the margin Winthrop penned the information that these men were "chosen by papers," which turned out to be nothing less than the secret ballot. No questions or recriminations for voting the "wrong" way.

Personal defeat gave John Winthrop a long-deserved rest, and sent him on his way toward a hero's place in history. Absolutely unbending when anybody or anything threatened the Bay Colony, Governor Winthrop set precedent by bowing immediately to the will of the people. He allowed power to pass to someone else, without violence, protest, or attempted reversion to the only kind of rule he had known in Europe for forty-two of his forty-six years of life—kingship, based on divine right.

The Bay settlers had reason for smug satisfaction over their first four years of sheer survival and mighty accomplishment. Then came September 18, 1634.

"Say No More"

Nature was coloring New England's September 1634 foliage, storing memories of beauty for the dark, blustery winter, when the *Griffin* docked at Boston harbor with double disaster aboard. The same ship brought to New England a royal demand for increased control over the Massachusetts Bay government, and forty-five-year-old Anne Hutchinson. Meanwhile, biding their time in the background, were the Pequot Indians.

No wonder the Puritans have come down in history as humorless. Though, occasionally, they did manage to break through their gloom with some well-placed irreverence. There was the time, for example, when general rejoicing and formal celebrations—including dinner at the Governor's table —greeted three of the colony's most famous newcomers, the highly articulate Puritan ministers Thomas Hooker, John Cotton, and Samuel Stone, who had narrowly escaped from English authorities. Some anonymous wit deflated ministerial dignity with the remark that the presence of Hooker, Cotton, and Stone should assure the destitute colony of fish, clothing, and building material.

The royal demand indicated that Charles and his newly promoted Archbishop of Canterbury William Laud—dubbed "The Shrimp" or "that little meddling hocus-pocus" by his enemies—had decided to shut off further escape to the New World, while bringing those already there under firm control. It had finally dawned on the King that Massachusetts Bay had grown into a refuge for nonconformists whose wealth, capacity for leadership, and working skills were lost to England.

At Laud's insistence, King Charles set up the Commission for Regulating Plantations, with Laud as its chairman. The Commission had the power to govern and pass laws for the colonies, remove colonial officers, change or revoke laws, and hear grievances of any kind from anybody dissatisfied with a colony. And as soon as Charles could find the time, he planned to send over a single governor general to take charge of all his far-flung American colonies—Massachusetts Bay, Plymouth, Virginia, Bermuda, and Barbados.

The King and Laud attracted some strange allies to their side from the Bay Colony. First there were the malcontents Christopher Gardner, Thomas Morton, and Philip Ratcliff—all banished from the colony for disruptive behavior, and all willing to give bitter testimony before the Privy Council in England.

Then there was Roger Williams, seemingly intent on smashing the fragile unity of the infant colony from within. Williams was a Cambridge-educated minister, not yet thirty, whose rapid speech barely kept pace with his brilliant mind. He was an ardent yet gentle dissenter from the Established Church who wrote to John Winthrop in 1632 of having been "persecuted in and out of my father's house these twenty years" (from about the age of eight). Amidst Charles's threatening noises, Williams raised centuries-long questions about white claims to Indian land, and about Church-State relations.

Somewhat inconsistently, he had emigrated to the New World, then proceeded to rebel against the King's granting Indian native land to the Puritans. The King's action was based on "a solemn public lie," he proclaimed, even though the Spanish, French, and Dutch regularly asserted that any Christian monarch had authority over lands discovered in his behalf, so long as they were not already occupied by Christians. Dissolve the colony and return all settlers to England, Williams insisted. Or at the very minimum send a letter to the King, pointing out His Majesty's implication in a horrendous lie, and demand that all reference to donation of land be omitted in the charter. Completely stumped by all this embarrassingly unanswerable talk, Governor Dudley and the General Court turned for help to Williams's fellow ministers. And the ministers were at least successful in convincing their brother to abandon his attacks on the charter.

In the end Williams himself insured his banishment from the colony when he moved from criticism of Indian policy to denunciation of the civil authorities. They must not be allowed to legislate on purely private matters, he contended. It was not their business to pass laws ordering church attendance or payment of a tax to support the church. And he advocated separating his own congregation at Salem from the one unified colony church, setting up instead an independent Salem church.

Late in 1635, the General Court ordered Roger Williams expelled from the colony after he had failed to repent his heresies. (The advantage of living in an almost empty land was that there was plenty of room for dissenters to establish themselves elsewhere.) Well aware that he could expect no mercy from the newly elected Governor John Haynes, Williams fled from Salem to find temporary shelter among the Indians. Former Governor Winthrop, who remained on friendly terms with Williams for the rest of his life, had warned Williams that he was about to be arrested and forcibly deported to England.

At first Williams had no place to settle permanently. Two years before, he and a few friends had attempted to establish themselves at Plymouth, where Governor William Bradford took note of Williams's "strange opinions" and described him as "a man godly and zealous, having many precious parts, but very unsettled in judgment." Knowing full well that they would be unwelcome in Plymouth a second time, Williams, his wife, and twenty devoted followers traveled on to the site of modern-day Providence, Rhode Island, where they purchased land from the Indians and laid the foundations for another New England colony in June 1636. Writing his autobiography thirty years later, Williams described his journey to Providence, during which he was "sorely tossed about for fourteen weeks in a bitter, winter season, not knowing what bread or board did mean."

Williams's inflammatory activities may have provoked John Endecott, his former parishioner, to cut the red cross of St. George, the dragon slayer, out of the royal flag. The old soldier denounced the cross as having been "given to the King of England by the Pope as an ensign of victory and so a superstitious thing and a relic of antichrist." This was almost too much for the General Court. Endecott's action could easily be made to appear official. After all, he was an early settler at Salem and the colony's first resident governor—royally appointed—and now served as Assistant in the General Court.

To separate themselves from Endecott's action, the rest of the General Court sentenced Endecott "for his rashness, uncharitableness, indiscretion, and exceeding the limits of his

John Endecott—Courtesy of the Secretary of the Commonwealth of Massachusetts. Photo by the author.

commission, to be sadly admonished, and also disabled for bearing any office in the commonwealth for the space of a year next ensuing." This light slap on the wrist was an attempt to appease the King, satisfy the colony, and yet show understanding of Endecott's excess of zeal. Meanwhile, even though living in fear of the King's next move, the company defiantly designed and flew its own special flag, a red banner with a plain white corner. Officials refused to display royal ensigns, except the one on Castle Island, which could easily be seen by English ships. "The master's mate in the Hector," John Winthrop reported, "spoke to some of our people aboard his ship that because we had not the King's colors at our fort, we were all traitors and rebels."

The sum of the colony's rebellious actions finally became too much for Charles. Their refusal to fly the royal flag was bad enough. Much worse because it was in writing had been the Freeman's Oath of April 1634, which promised citizen support for the colony, conspicuously omitting allegiance to the King. Charles retaliated, issuing additional orders designed to make it difficult if not impossible for Puritans to leave England. "Their only end," he contended, "is to live as much as they can without the reach of authority."

Charles was absolutely correct, though his new restrictions had little effect. The King had too many problems in England to enforce his anti-emigration edicts. But New Englanders had too many overlapping crises to enjoy their life of independence. At the same time that Roger Williams was being banished and Endecott carefully silenced, Anne Hutchinson was making her way front and center. The magistrates (governor, deputy governor, and assistants) all quavered before America's first woman intellectual, who narrowly missed demolishing the colony. Daughter of a dissenting vicar in Lincolnshire, England, she had married a well-to-do neighbor, William Hutchinson, who indulged her every whim, including her insistence on carting him and all but the oldest of their thirteen children off to the New World.

She used her intense intelligence to study and interpret the one book available to her, the Bible. And from her reading she evolved a complex theology, maintaining that a person could experience his or her own salvation, and would be "filled with God" after conversion to this new experience. With supreme confidence she outtalked and outreasoned any opponent, male or female, while her loving, loyal husband looked on admiringly. Like an old-fashioned misogynist or modern male chauvinist, John Winthrop, who himself proved no match for Mrs. Hutchinson's intellect, pitied William Hutchinson as "a man of very weak parts and wholly guided by his wife."

Anne Hutchinson's religious ideas, her opponents agreed, would overthrow both Church and State. Her pronouncement that each person had a private relationship with God could easily incite individuals to act above and beyond the law. In fact, within two years of her arrival, she had divided the colony into hostile camps. On one side were her powerful supporters—all of Boston's merchants and residents, with five notable exceptions including John Wilson, the pastor (she and her followers once showed their contempt by walking out in the middle of his sermon) and John Winthrop. On the other side, in fierce opposition, were most of the other towns and churches.

She had begun innocently enough. Noting that male members of the Boston church met by themselves to discuss the minister's sermons, she started to hold similar meetings at her home—directly across the street from the Winthrops—sometimes twice a week, for as many as 100 women. As a woman she was never allowed to preach in church, but soon she attracted both men and women to her home where she would discourse at length on theology. Edward Johnson, New England's enthusiastic historian and eyewitness, quotes one of her admirers (a man): " 'Come along with me. . . . I'll bring you to a woman that preaches better gospel than any of your black coats that have been at the ninneversity.' " Then, damning her with fulsome praise, her admirer turns anti-intellectual, inadvertently illustrating the problem troubling many of her opponents: " 'For my part,' saith he, 'I had rather hear such a one that speaks from the mere motion of the spirit, without any study at all, than any of your learned scholars, although they may be fuller of Scripture.' "

Boston's scholarly forty-nine-year-old minister, John Cot-

Sir Henry Vane, the Younger—Courtesy of the Secretary of the Commonwealth of Massachusetts. Photo by the author.

ton, blew hot and cold on the subject of his star pupil (it was his migration to the New World that caused her own). Throughout the controversy, this short, dumpy man, with the ruddy face and cheerful disposition, alternated between mild private encouragement and public pronouncements vague enough to keep himself out of trouble.

Much more enthusiastic was twenty-three-year-old Henry Vane, wealthy Puritan graduate of Oxford, who arrived in Boston late in 1635, and six months later became the third man to defeat John Winthrop for the governorship. Elected on a pro-Hutchinson platform he brought Anne Hutchinson's opinions into the council chamber where he supported her strongly. Young Vane was the son of the powerful royalist Sir Henry Vane, comptroller and ambassador for King Charles, and a favorite of Queen Henrietta Maria. The new governor's youth and family connections made him suspect in the Bay Colony, even though he had proclaimed his rebellion against his father by calling himself a staunch Puritan.

After one year in office, he was ousted in the hotly contested election of 1637, which the anti-Hutchinsonians slyly moved to Cambridge to lessen the number of Bostonians present and voting. "There was great danger of tumult," John Winthrop explained in his journal, describing that election day. He told of "fierce speeches," and noted that "some laid hands on others." John Winthrop, candidate of the "white coats" as the conservatives were called, defeated the "blue coat" incumbent Governor Vane. Sullenly, Boston took revenge by refusing to supply the usual honor guards to escort the Governor to the opening meeting of the General Court. "The former governor never had less than four," Winthrop noted without comment.

Vane returned to England where, despite his father's position, he openly challenged the King, and achieved immortality in a sonnet by Puritan poet John Milton, which begins:

> Vane, young in years, but in sage counsels old.

And Edward Johnson, who had been on the opposite side in the Hutchinson controversy, mellowed enough by the early 1650s to dedicate one of his homespun poems to him, this one titled, "Sir Henry Vane, once Governor of the English people in New England":

> The parents, Vane, of worthy fame, in Christ and thou for him
> Through ocean wide in new world tried a while his warriors bin
> With small defeat thou didst retreat to Britain ground again,
> There stand thou stout, for Christ hold out, Christ's champion ay remain.

One of John Winthrop's first moves as Vane's successor in the office of governor was to announce the summoning of the General Court to Cambridge, where he deliberately kept it until the end of the Hutchinson controversy. As a result of the Watertown protest, the court now included magistrates as well as deputies representing the towns. And the court had expanded powers. It now passed, administered, and enforced laws, when in session. The role of the governor had evolved into carrying out the will of the court, and serving as moderator of public assemblies.

To the surprise of no one, the court, with Governor Winthrop presiding, decided to try Anne Hutchinson for sedition (conduct or words aiming to incite discontent against the government) and for contempt of the magistrates. She had already been excommunicated from the Church.

The proceedings—they can hardly be called a trial—lasted for two days. The court, consisting of about forty members with the clergy also present, had already prejudged the Hutchinsonians, but was going through the motions of upholding John Winthrop's "due form of government" under law. Anne Hutchinson successfully parried. all attempts to shake her beliefs.

Heady with victory as they trounced all opposition, the Hutchinsonians sank into an anti-intellectual mysticism. They alone were the saints and the judges, everyone else the sinners and the judged. Mrs. Hutchinson herself claimed "prophetical inspiration," a series of divine revelations, including that she "should come into New England and should here be persecuted." Therefore, she warned: "Take heed what you go about to do unto me . . . for I know that for this you go about to do to me, God will ruin you and your posterity, and this whole state."

Succinctly, Winthrop observed that Anne Hutchinson's runaway tongue produced her own downfall: "The Court and all the rest of the Assembly (except those of her own party) did observe a special providence of God that . . . her own mouth should deliver her into the power of the Court, as guilty of that which all suspected her for, but were not furnished with proof sufficient to proceed against her."

The sentence was banishment from the colony, "as being a woman not fit for our society."

Anne Hutchinson protested: "I desire to know wherefore I am banished."

"Say no more," retorted Governor Winthrop. "The Court knows wherefore and is satisfied."

Some sixty colonists from Boston and about twenty from neighboring towns were also banished, and departed for Rhode Island. The internal menace the Hutchinsonians presented to Massachusetts Bay was too much to bear at a time when the King—two times in the three years of Anne Hutchinson's residence there—was demanding the return of the charter and threatening actual invasion. Governor Winthrop justified the banishment as being "most for the glory of God" and for "public peace." He contended: "Those brethren were so divided from the rest of the country in their judgment and practice, as it could not stand with the public peace that they should continue amongst us."

On the other hand, a sympathetic but anonymous balladeer put words loaded with pathos into the mouth of Anne Hutchinson as she was driven from Massachusetts with her huge family:

Home, home—where's my baby's home?
Here we seek, there we seek my baby's home to find.

Come, come, come, my baby, come!
We found her home, we lost her home, and home is far
behind.
Come, my baby, come!
Find my baby's home!

To prevent a recurrence of the Hutchinson affair, the
court sharply restricted immigration into the colony. Dissenters who had already arrived would be granted only enough
time to find habitation outside the commonwealth. Thus on
the American side of the Atlantic, Hutchinsonian sympathizers were refused entry, while on the English side, Puritans
were technically forbidden to depart.

"Want Therefore Shall Not I"

Actually, New Englanders got their way on both sides of the ocean. They succeeded in keeping out undesirables at the same time that Winthrop was able to observe in his journal, June 5, 1638: "Many ships arrived this year, with people of good quality and estate, notwithstanding the council's order that none such should come without the King's license." He explained that the King and his council had so many other troubles that "they had neither heart nor leisure to look after the affairs of New England." Quite pleased with the lofty caliber of New England settlers, the Governor noted that other English colonies had to depend on impressment for peopling their areas, whereas "men of all conditions, rich and poor, servants and others, offered themselves readily for New England."

When John Winthrop wrote of rich men anxious to emigrate to New England, he probably included William Fiennes, first Viscount Saye and Sele (Lord Saye for short), who almost became one of the colony's prize catches. At the age of fifty-four, Lord Saye belonged to one of England's oldest and most distinguished families, and was one of the few Puritan noblemen in the House of Lords. Back in 1629, as a member of the Puritan inner circle, which met at the Sempringham estate of his son-in-law the Earl of Lincoln, he had taken great interest in the New England venture. From the beginning he had given the colony strong financial support. Lately, a thought, which may always have been at the back of his mind, had pushed itself forward as a plea to create a permanent and hereditary nobility in the Bay Colony. In return, he, his wealth, and several of his noble friends—including Robert Grenville, second Count Brooke, a twenty-eight-year-old Puritan colleague in the House of Lords—would graciously consent to emigrate. Familiar with the Renaissance royal courts of Europe, he apparently had no conception of the endless struggle to snatch a living from the wilderness, or of the difficulty of creating a workable government, with the hindrances felt from both inside and out.

Lord Saye's overtures to the Bay Colony arrived amidst the troubles with Roger Williams and Anne Hutchinson, compounded by royal threats to revoke the charter. This probably explains the willingness of the General Court to meet Lord Saye halfway by establishing a "Council for Life." John Winthrop and his supporters convinced themselves of the need for rule by a strong body of magistrates. Accordingly, the court provided for the election, as demand arose, of "a certain number of magistrates for the term of their lives as a standing council, not to be removed but upon conviction of crime, insufficiency, or for some other weighty cause; the Governor for the time being to be always president of this council." The principle of life tenure lasted exactly three years—finally repudiated by the deputies, representing the more democratic tendencies of the towns where the people actually lived instead of the capital where the magistrates spent a great deal of time.

In this short-lived flirtation with a permanent ruling clique, the Bay Colony devised some long-lasting political practice. The idea that high government officials could and should be removed for specific cause found its way paraphrased and updated—into two sections of the United States Constitution. Article II, Section 4: "The president, vice-president, and all civil officers of the United States shall be removed from office on impeachment for, and conviction of, treason, bribery, or other high crimes and misdemeanors." And Article III, Section I: "The judges, both of the supreme and inferior courts, shall hold their offices during good behavior." In practice, federal judges remain on the bench for life, unless impeached and convicted of crimes which constitute other than "good behavior."

The negotiations with Lord Saye produced a sharply focused picture of the actual working of the Massachusetts Bay government. John Cotton, who in the three years since his arrival had become the commonwealth's preeminent spokesman for New England Puritanism, was given the delicate task of convincing Lord Saye to accept the council for life in place of a permanent and hereditary nobility. At the same time Cotton had to portray the colony attractively enough to entice prestigious emigrants such as Viscount Saye and Sele and Count Brooke.

Poor Cotton. It took some 320 years of misinterpretation—though apparently Lord Saye understood quite well, for he bypassed the chance to settle in Massachusetts Bay—before the Reverend's most quotable lines were finally returned to the context of their own time (seventeenth century), place (unsettled frontier), and reason for writing (to encourage the physical presence, or at least the continued financial support of wealthy Puritan nobles). Cotton's words—intended as a description of an ideal and stable self-government, which would then overcome nobleman Saye's fear of too much democracy —have been quoted far and wide to prove his own and the colony's oligarchic tendencies. In answer to Lord Saye's inquiry he wrote: "Democracy I do not conceive that ever God did ordain as a fit government either for church or commonwealth. If the people be governors, who shall be governed?"

In 1954, B. Katherine Brown toppled the traditional view of Cotton's so-called antidemocratic tendencies, pointing out in her monograph "The Puritan Concept of Aristocracy" that "Cotton defined aristocracy by how many ruled, not by how those rulers came to power." She elaborated: "Puritan aristocracy bears a stong resemblance to our modern democracy. Officials were elected by the people and given authority to rule. . . . Wealth and heredity carried no weight in government. . . ." And in Massachusetts, she pointed out, the Puritan concept of aristocracy stressed "a sense of moral obligation on the part of the rulers, . . . a factor which has generally been pushed aside in the modern definition of the word."

Redeemed after centuries of libel and slander, Cotton's further explanation of the Bay Colony government is a fair description of the present United States government. Cotton wrote: "Though it be a popular state, where a people choose their own governors, yet the government is not a democracy, if it be administered, not by the people, but by the governors, whether one (for then it is a monarchy, though elective) or by many, for then (as you know) it is an aristocracy." The United States government today, then, is an "aristocracy." The system combines choice by the people of their own state governors and President, who administer the government, together with state and national legislatures (also chosen by the people), and with the state and national courts (indirectly chosen by the people through their elected leaders and representatives).

The John Cotton–Lord Saye correspondence, and the short-lived Council for Life were intellectual exercises compared to the Bay Colony's usual life-or-death emergencies all through the 1630s. Especially during the years 1634–1638, crises and troubles seemed to erupt fast, furiously, and often simultaneously. Thus the magistrates had no sooner expelled Roger Williams than they were embroiled with Anne Hutchinson. And during the Hutchinsonian controversy they had to face their first major confrontation with the Indians.

Most of the fighting in this so-called Pequot War took place in the brand new settlement of Connecticut. Hostility between the Pequots and other New England Indians probably saved the English colonists from extinction. The Massachusetts, Mohegans, Narragansetts, and the River tribes all readily allied themselves with Connecticut, the Bay Colony, Plymouth, and Rhode Island. Together they battled to curb the powerful Pequots, accusing the tribe of forcible intrusion into New England, and sporadic murders of Indians as well as whites.

In Massachusetts Bay the Puritans had generally observed punctiliously correct relations with the local Indians. Alden Vaughan, a modern student of Indian-Puritan relations quotes the company's advice to Governor Endecott, a full year before the arrival of the Winthrop group: "If any of the savages pretend right of inheritance to all or any part of the lands granted . . . in our patent, we pray you endeavor to purchase their title, that we may avoid the least scruple of intrusion." On the basis of extensive research Vaughan concludes: "There is no evidence that this policy was ever violated." But foreign intruders—those Pequots, of course—almost ruined this good relationship between local Indians and English colonists.

Self-defense rather than land-grabbing may have been the Puritan rationale for the war, but extermination of the Pequots made unlimited Puritan expansion possible in New England. "Divine slaughter," Reverend Thomas Shepard of Cambridge called the killing of every Pequot in sight. And any Pequots still alive after the two-month battle, May 26–July 28, 1637, was over were sold into slavery. As a result of this short, decisive encounter, the balance of power shifted to favor the English colonists over the native Indians, who were more numerous, but less organized and less effectively armed.

Along with their unquestionably admirable legacies to the future, the Puritans were now also able to bequeath the doubtfully moral mission of westward expansion—all the way across the North American continent by mid-nineteenth century, and across the Pacific in the nineteenth and twentieth centuries. In fact, the earliest missionary to Hawaii, in 1820, was Hiram Bingham of Boston, a Congregational minister. The Congregationalists were the direct descendants of the Puritans.

Following the Pequot War, the General Court in 1638 took steps to prevent the establishment of a standing group of military men, who might easily, in John Winthrop's words, "overthrow the civil power." They allowed the ancestor of the Ancient and Honorable Artillery to come into being, but made it subordinate to civilian authority. (This civilian control of the military appeared later in the United States Constitution, Article I, Section 8: "The congress shall have the power . . . to raise and support armies . . ., to provide and maintain a navy." This power is shared with another civilian. Article II, Section 2: "The President shall be commander in chief of the army and navy of the United States.")

Politically, the Pequot war had meant conducting foreign relations without royal supervision. Furthermore, the wartime cooperation of scattered towns and settlements in supplying men and arms provided the first stirrings of colonial unity.

Meanwhile, these same years, so crowded with discouraging dissension, war, and royal threats saw the origins of the Eastern Establishment in the United States. In 1635 the Massachusetts Puritans hired Philemon Pormont as schoolmaster in Roxbury, which led within the next few years to the opening of the first public school in America. In 1636 they founded Harvard College, and two years after that set up the first printing press in English North America (the Spaniards in Mexico had operated a printing press since 1539).

These actions sparkle brilliantly against the assertion of royal governor Sir William Berkeley of Virginia in 1671: "I thank God there are no free schools nor printing . . . for learning has brought disobedience and heresy and sects into the world, and printing has divulged them, and libels against the best government. God keep us from them both!" Virginians made sporadic attempts at public schooling, but were badly hindered by the wide scattering of settlers in contrast to New Englanders, who huddled together in towns built around the church-meeting house.

Printer Stephen Daye, an indentured servant trained to operate the new Cambridge press, turned out as his first publication a broadside sheet containing the Freeman's Oath. This was followed shortly afterward by the Bay Psalm Book, intended as an easy-to-sing version of God's word. The learned ministers John Eliot and Thomas Welde of Roxbury, and Richard Mather of Dorchester, produced some unique translations; for example the Twenty-third Psalm:

The Lord to me a shepherd is, want therefore shall
    not I.
He in the folds of tender grass, doth cause me down
    to lie:
To waters calm me gently leads. Restore my soul
    doth he.
He doth in paths of righteousness, for his name's
    sake lead me.
Yea though in the valley of death's shade I walk,
    none ill I'll fear:
Because thou are with me, thy rod, and staff my
    comfort are
For me a table thou hast spread, in presence of my
    foes.
Thou dost anoint my head with oil, my cup it over-
    flows.
Goodness and mercy surely shall all my days follow
    me:
And in the Lord's house I shall dwell so long as days
    shall be.*

* The King James version:

    The Lord is my shepherd; I shall not want.
    He maketh me to lie down in green pastures;
    He leadeth me beside the still waters.
    He restoreth my soul;
    He leadeth me in the paths of righteousness for His name's sake.
    Yea, though I walk through the valley of the shadow of death,
    I will fear no evil,
    For Thou art with me;
    Thy rod and Thy staff, they comfort me.
    Thou preparest a table before me in the presence of mine enemies;
    Thou anointest my head with oil; my cup runneth over.
    Surely goodness and mercy shall follow me all the days of my life;
    And I shall dwell in the house of the Lord for ever.

Again, out popped the Puritan sense of ridicule, directed at highly respected ministers. This time the author was himself a minister, Thomas Shepard, a clerical founder of Massachusetts Bay and pastor of the First Church of Cambridge:

> You Roxb'ry poets, keep clear of the crime
> Of missing to give us very good rhyme.
> And you of Dorchester, your verses lengthen,
> But with the text's own words, you will them
>   strengthen.

They had more time for small humor now and then as their first decade in Massachusetts Bay came to an end. Their population, which began with a thousand adventurous souls, was now approaching fifteen thousand. They had learned to feed, shelter, and govern themselves. Prosperity had come with the constant arrivals of shiploads of settlers, requiring basic necessities. And they had developed their own shipbuilding industry on a small but growing scale. Returning visitors to England brought glowing accounts of life in New England, leading an Englishman to observe enviously: "When a New England man returns home, how he is looked after, entertained; the ground he walks on beloved for his sake, and the house held better where he is. How are his words listened to, laid up and related when he is gone. Neither is any love or kindness too much for such a man."

A New England woman returning home should also have been the subject of considerable envy. If she was not yet a full partner in marriage, she had at least assumed the role of self-sufficient helpmate, a steep step above European seventeenth-century marital servitude. In her wilderness home she had the life-preserving responsibility for maintaining family well-being with a constant supply of food, medicine, and clothing. In addition, the fact that there were fewer women than men in the colony—exactly the opposite was true in Europe—made colony officials frown publicly on wife-beating, and work constantly to refine laws insuring adequate financial support for married women and widows.

Politically, though women were not considered "freemen" and hence not citizens, at least one of their number, fifty-year-old Elizabeth Poole, reached hitherto unheard-of heights. In 1639, she founded and became the leader of the town of Taunton, Massachusetts. Sad to say, there is such scanty information on her political career that her future biographer will have to work from vivid imagination instead of solid research. John Winthrop's journal reports only: "This year a plantation was begun at Tecticutt by a gentlewoman, an ancient maid, one Mrs. Poole. She went late thither and endured much hardship and lost much cattle." Aside from this entry and English records reporting that Mistress Poole was born in Taunton, Somerset, England, in 1589, and was a member in 1623 of the company of Dorchester Adventurers all the rest of the facts about her life are contained on her tombstone:

A native of England, of good family, friends and prospect, all of which she left in the prime of her life to enjoy the religion of her conscience in this distant wilderness. A great proprietor of the township of Taunton, a chief promoter of its settlement in 1639. Having employed the opportunity of her virgin state in piety, liberality, and sanctity of manners, she died aged 65.

There is even disagreement as to whether Elizabeth Poole was ever married. The prefix "Mrs." which Winthrop placed before her name was used as a title of distinction for socially prominent females, whether single or married. Records exist of girls, ages six and seven, addressed as "Mrs." in this period.

Relaxed about their future, the Bay Puritans ignored Archbishop Laud's repeated order to send the charter back to England for review. The King was too far away for meaningful supervision, but if he got his hands on the charter he might seek to impose a royally appointed governor on Massachusetts Bay, as he had done in Virginia. So they procrastinated, invented all kinds of excuses for not returning the charter to England, rounded up highly placed supporters already in England to appeal to the King, and sent trusted messengers back across the Atlantic to plead their case.

They never won their argument, but neither did they lose their charter. A procession of crises at home kept the King too busy to bother about a worthless wilderness 3,000 miles away.

The same procession of crises derailed the Bay Colony from its straight path to utopia.

"Popish Soap"

Under Charles I, Englishmen first fled, then bled. And all the while, their King's most positive achievement was to assemble one of the world's great collections of Western painting.

On commission of the King, Peter Paul Rubens, who was in London as ambassador from the Spanish Netherlands, painted *The Blessings of Peace*, celebrating the conclusion of a peace treaty between England and Spain. Gratefully, the King knighted Rubens in 1630, the same year he accepted tribute in verse from Richard Fanshawe who described England as

> ... one blest isle
> Which in a sea of plenty swam
> And turtles sang on ev'ry bough
> A safe retreat to all that came
> As ours is now.

Two years later, in 1632, Charles appointed Anthony Van Dyck, early pupil of Rubens and portrait painter from Antwerp, as "Principal Painter in ordinary to their Majesties." In return for an annual pension of £200, a studio at Blackfriars, and a knighthood, Van Dyck remained in England for the final nine years of his life. With the help of studio assistants, he painted some 350 portraits of royalty and aristocracy, bequeathing to the world an impression of magnificence at Charles's court.

Sycophancy replaced talent as poets fell over themselves to crown this impression of magnificence by depicting a blissful, happy, peace-endowed England. One court poet, Thomas Carew, chanted:

> But let us that in myrtle bowers sit
> Under secure shades, use the benefit
> Of peace and plenty, which the blessed hand
> Of our good King gives this obdurate land.

Even one of England's literary giants, sixty-year-old Ben Jonson, actor, dramatist, and poet since the last years of Elizabeth, looking for favor in his last years, intoned:

> Indeed, when had Great Britain greater cause
> Than now to love the sovereign and the laws?

But far away in Rome and secure in his reputation as Europe's foremost baroque sculptor and architect, Giovanni Lorenzo Bernini, felt no need to frame his words and thoughts to please the King of England. A "doomed" man was his reaction when he received Van Dyck's 1637 painting, *Charles I in Three Positions*, from which he had been commissioned to execute a bust of the King: "Never have I beheld features more unfortunate."

Actually, though peace with Spain and France had finally

come in the 1630s, bliss and happiness had not followed—
either for the King or for his subjects. More from arrogant indifference than from purposeful malice, the King took steps
that antagonized every segment of English society. Early in
his reign, his apparent abolition of Parliament in March 1629
had started an eleven-year exodus of the country's politically
intellectual nonconformists, the Puritans.

Next, the King antagonized the growing class of merchants
who had remained in England. Despite Parliament's refusal,
1625–1629, to grant him the usual royal privilege for life to
levy tonnage and poundage, he proclaimed these duties solely
by royal authority. Those refusing payment faced imprisonment either by the Royal Council or by the Star Chamber.

In short order the Star Chamber itself became a cause for
revolt. Like benevolences, the poetically named forced loans,
the Star Chamber sounded innocuous. Its name came from the
gold-painted stars on the ceiling of the main room in the
King's Palace of Westminster, where the Privy Council and
judges of this court met together. Its jurisdiction was vague,
pro-royal, and powerful enough to inflict any penalties short
of death. The Tudors had used the Star Chamber—no jury
trial was necessary there—whenever they needed quick and
effective enforcement of royal prerogative. (This court made
such a lasting impression that it finds its way, without capital
letters and as an adjective, in modern English-language news-
paper and magazine accounts of arbitrary and secret proceedings, and is carefully defined in the most recent edition of
Webster's unabridged dictionary: "of, relating to, constitut-
ing, or in the manner of a secret oppressive or irresponsible
judicial body.")

Richard Chambers was one of the first victims of Charles's
Star Chamber for his refusal to submit to tonnage and poundage duties. Little is known about him except his "insolent man-

ner" in uttering "undutiful, seditious, and false words" (the official description of his manner on trial) when he told his inquisitors: "The merchants are in no part of the world so screwed and wrung as in England; in Turkey they have more encouragement." The Star Chamber ruled that "the words spoke were a comparing of His Majesty's government with the government of the Turks, intending thereby to make the people believe that His Majesty's happy government may be termed Turkish tyranny." His punishment was an enormous fine of £2,000 and imprisonment for six years.

By 1637, the Star Chamber had gone from attempted enforcement of the King's tax levies to strict censorship of all printed material—books, pamphlets, newsletters, and plays. At the same time that Anne Hutchinson was attacking the established (Puritan) church of the Bay Colony, three dissenters in England published violent attacks against Archbishop Laud and his bishops. The three were John Bastwick, a doctor; Henry Burton, a clergyman; and William Prynne, a lawyer. The Star Chamber condemned them to be pilloried, to have their ears cut off, and to spend their life in solitary confinement. In addition, Prynne's cheeks were branded S. L.—for "seditious libeler" of Laud. All three men were put into the pillories in the palace yard, where to the crowds who came to taunt or pity, they proclaimed their continued faith in Jesus, and in the legal precedents and ancient liberties of all Englishmen. When a hangman sawed off Prynne's ears, a horrified roar resounded in the courtyard. Laud's unfeeling reaction was to present a new play to the King at Christ Church Hall, Oxford, mocking the Puritans. One of the characters represented Prynne with his ears cut off.

But the barbarity had no effect on twenty-one-year-old John Lilburne when he was hauled before the Star Chamber exactly six months later. He refused to retract his strong statements on English liberty. Born a gentleman and affectionately nicknamed "freeborn John," he was whipped all the way from the Fleet Street prison to the Palace yard, pilloried, and starved almost to the point of death in prison.

With these well-publicized examples of torture, the King used the mere threat of Star Chamber proceedings to collect other imaginatively revived taxes. After taking on the merchants by levying tonnage and poundage, Charles turned to the landed gentry, forcing members to accept knighthoods at an exorbitant cost, or pay an even higher fine for refusal. For the peerage he conceived "forest laws." On the pretext that the King had eternal title to all forest land, current owners who had cleared the land faced heavy fines.

And to show that he had not forgotten the ordinary man, he extracted great sums of money through a new kind of monopoly, this time on the manufacture of soap. One corporation of soap-boilers paid the King a royalty of £4 per ton for all soap it manufactured. In return, the corporation was allowed to test all soap produced in England, and could condemn at will—in the pretended interests of purity—all soap manufactured by nonjoiners. Someone started a whispering campaign, alleging that Roman Catholics had a large degree of control over the new company. "Popish soap," people screamed. This soap "would certainly corrupt the body and might also corrupt the soul." Of course, the real anxiety was that the same principle of granting monopolies would be extended to all sorts of companies, allowing only a select group of favored merchants to succeed in business—exactly what happened very soon.

But probably Charles's most infamous scheme was "ship money." Always, English kings had the right to require seaport towns to supply ships for purposes of defense. Now, Charles extended requests to inland towns, and asked for money rather than ships. But he acted at a time when there was no war, and so no war emergency. Consequently, the King had to work at rousing enough war fever to make his request for ship money seem legitimate. He had his courtiers go up and down the country warning darkly of the need to insure naval supremacy over the Dutch.

The problem was that he had chosen the wrong enemy. As Calvinist Protestants, the Dutch were in close agreement with the King's Puritan opponents. Therefore, war—and money for war—would be acceptable to the Puritans only (1) if declared against the Spanish or Austrian Catholics, (2) after consultation with Parliament, and (3) with tax money duly voted by Parliament.

Edward Hyde, the Earl of Clarendon, the royalist who in the 1660s wrote one of the best histories of this earlier period, in an attempt to purge the monarchy of rottenness, hyphenated *ship-money* and called it "a word of lasting sound in the memory of this kingdom." Clarendon described the ominous results:

> After the continued receipt of ship-money for four years together, it was at last (upon the refusal of a private gentleman to pay thirty shillings as his share) with great solemnity publicly argued before all the judges of England in the exchequer chamber, and by the major part of them, the King's right to impose asserted, and the tax adjudged lawful.

The lesson, which Clarendon drew was that the "judgment proved of more advantage and credit to the gentleman condemned (Mr. Hampden) than to the King's service."

Early in 1638, when the case was heard before twelve judges, seven voted in favor of the King. But more significantly, five judges upheld John Hampden. Two judges in the minority based their decision on strong constitutional grounds. They found that writs for ship money were nothing more nor less than taxes imposed by the King without Parliamentary consent. Three judges, apparently in sympathy but not bold enough to stand up to the King on constitutional grounds, joined the two minority opponents on purely technical grounds—that the defendant had been summoned to provide a ship or a ship part, not money to purchase a ship.

Speaking for the seven-man majority, royalist Chief Justice John Lord Finch almost killed the royal prerogative with excessive subservience. Englishmen's property, he asserted, was not their own but the king's: "Acts of Parliament to take away his royal power in the defense of the kingdom are void. They are void acts of Parliament to bind the King not to command the subjects, their persons and goods, and I say their money too, for no acts of Parliament make any difference." This was the same John Finch speaking who had been forcibly held in the Speaker's Chair as he attempted to support the King's 1629 adjournment of Parliament.

In the end, by completely ignoring Parliament and its stubbornly proclaimed "ancient prerogatives," Charles acquired a tainted reputation for breaking the law at will. Furthermore, the narrow court victory for the King proved to be the first brake on his arbitrary disposition of his subjects' liberty and property. The King won the immediate case at hand, but again, as in the Darnel case of 1627, the opposition gained excellent publicity—and ammunition to trigger support for their cause in the coming civil war. They had only to repeat verbatim the Chief Justice's words.

Hero of the ship-money case was the very rich John Hampden who, as Clarendon noted, fought the payment of a mere thirty shillings. Born at the end of the previous century in

1594, when Elizabeth Tudor still reigned, John Hampden began opposing the Stuarts, first in James's Parliament of 1621, and then in Charles's Parliaments of 1625–1629. A persuasive speaker and able leader, he was one of the twenty-seven members of Parliament imprisoned for refusal to pay the forced loan of 1626, but released before the reconvening of the Parliament of 1628.

He had never forgiven Charles for imprisonment of John Eliot after the violent dissolution of Parliament in 1629, blaming this imprisonment for Eliot's death in 1632. Eliot's children, who were left in Hampden's care, were a constant reminder to him of Eliot's fate, and intensified his own opposition to the King.

As the King bumbled about, inciting political opposition, his Archbishop Laud was equally busy rousing religious discontent. Laud's persecution caused an increasing number of ministers to emigrate to New England. In the beginning almost no ministers had gone, leading some future students of the Puritan migration to suppose that the initial impetus was more political than religious. But by 1633, Laud's attempt first to silence and then to capture and imprison John Cotton, William Hooker, and Samuel Stone, sent three of England's most famous ministers permanently to New England. They succeeded in escaping to Massachusetts Bay only by deceiving Laud as to the port from which they finally departed.

Despite the royal regulations aimed at making emigration impossible, or at least very difficult, there was no appreciable decrease in the number of political and religious Puritans fleeing to New England. Fortunately for New England the regulations were strict but the enforcement decidedly lax.

At one time, John Pym and Oliver Cromwell, two men who eventually led the opposition to Charles, thought of emigrat-

Reade in this Image him, whose dearest blood
Is thought noe price to buy his Countryes good,
Whose name shall flourish, till the blast of ffame
Shall want a Trumpet, or true Worth, a name.
Edw: Bower pinxit   G: Glouer fecit

Contemporary engraving of John Pym by John Glover—Courtesy of the Trustees of the British Museum, London.

ing. There was no Parliamentary channel for complaint. No protest such as the Watertown outcry in the Bay Colony had been heard. Throughout England, Puritan lecturers attempting to sound a cry of dissent and discontent were silenced—sometimes imprisoned, sometimes driven to self-exile in Holland or New England.

Pym and Cromwell finally decided to remain in England, but another Puritan, Thomas Shepard, thirty-year-old minister and friend of Cotton, Hooker, and Stone, decided to emigrate in 1635. In his memoirs he cited the Puritan idea of a "calling," the sacred duty to use God-given talent—exactly as John Winthrop had done: "I saw that this time could not be long without trouble from King Charles, and I saw no reason to spend my time privately, when I might possibly exercise my talent publicly in New England."

Shepard witnessed England's troubles in the 1630s and decided to flee. Edward Hyde, Earl of Clarendon, the moderate royalist who opposed kingly excesses, watched the same troubles, decided to remain—and looking back from the 1660s found some praise for the early years of Charles's reign. He lambasted Buckingham and ship money, but recorded that by 1639, when King Charles was almost forty, "England enjoyed the greatest measure of felicity that it had ever known." He contrasted England with the rest of Europe, wracked for the past two decades by still another series of religious and civil wars.

Only the King of England, Clarendon gloated, "seemed to be seated upon that pleasant promontory, that might safely view the tragic sufferings of all his neighbors about him, without any other concernment than what arose from his own princely heart and Christian compassion, to see such desolation wrought by the pride, and passion, and ambition of private persons, supported by princes who knew not what themselves would have."

Clarendon pointed out that Charles had not one but three kingdoms—England, Ireland, and Scotland. His navy commanded the seas and brought great wealth from trade, and his overseas colonies were flourishing. Then Clarendon concluded dramatically:

A small, scarce discernible cloud arose in the north, which was shortly after attended with such a storm that never gave over raging till it had shaken and even rooted up, the greatest and tallest cedars of the three nations; blasted all its beauty and fruitfulness; brought its strength to decay, and its glory to reproach and almost to desolation.

That "scarce discernible cloud" was Scotland. Charles, like his father James I, was King of both England and Scotland, but no formal political union had ever been legislated. Now Charles and Archbishop Laud determined to impose the Episcopal hierarchy of England on Scotland. Uniting the two countries was all-important. The English had not achieved union by the political act of crowning James VI of Scotland as James I of Great Britain. Therefore, Charles and Laud would work up to union through religion, by combining the Churches of the two Britains, England and Scotland.

The Presbyterian order of Scotland had taken deep root in that country since its founding there by John Knox in 1560. So when the King tried to force the Scots into the English Church, they replied with the National Covenant of 1638. And vast numbers of Scotsmen swore to defend their traditional political and religious rights.

In mid-1638 Charles decided to take Scotland by force of arms. Confident that he could make all decisions on war and peace by himself—and raise money without having to grovel to Parliament—the King tried raising an army of 40,000, but succeeded in raising one of only 14,000. "Our army is weak," protested Sir Edmund Verney, one of Charles's courtiers. "Our purse is weaker, and if we fight with these forces and early in the year, we shall have our throats cut, and to delay fighting long we cannot for want of money to keep our army together."

Charles's army of stragglers was soundly defeated by the aroused Scots, using men, boys, and women to defend their homes. And even this muddled attempt to subdue Scotland broke Charles financially and forced him to make peace. Determined to force union on Scotland by outright conquest if necessary, Charles called Parliament into session in April 1640 for financial help. Balladmonger Martin Parker, who had been writing since the reign of James I, reflected popular expectation of a better England:

> This happy April will, I trust,
> Give all true subjects reason just
> Of joy to feel a pleasant gust,
> To yield them heart's content:
> For we may be assured by this
> If anything hath been amiss,
> Our King and State will all redress
> In this good Parliament.

With no success in Scotland, Archbishop Laud who had long advocated suppressing that troublesome Presbyterian country, quickly lost his position of Charles's chief adviser to Thomas Wentworth. This was the same Thomas Wentworth who had been the King's opponent in the Parliaments of 1625–1628, and had been imprisoned for several months after refusing to pay the forced loan of 1626. A middle-of-the-road moderate, Wentworth had returned to Parliament in 1628, where he supported the Petition of Right. But by the summer of 1628 he had switched sides, accepting a baronetcy from the King—and from 1633–1639, with Charles's blessing, had ruled the colony of Ireland as a virtual king. He had acquired for himself the enormous yearly income of £13,000, making him one of England's wealthiest men. By 1639, the King had made him the Earl of Strafford, giving Wentworth an honor he had long craved. The Puritans immediately titled him Black Tom, the Tyrant. They had visions of an invasion from Ireland, with the newly created earl at the head of an Irish army.

Laud and Wentworth agreed on the strong necessity for absolutism in the monarchy, but differed in their methods of achieving it. Fussy, short-tempered, and scholarly, Laud wanted a return to the medieval Church of England—but with the King instead of the Pope at its head. The Church would control every segment of society, without dissent. Wentworth, ambitious and formidable, was twenty years younger than Laud but gazed out at the world with a ravaged face set atop a heavy body twisted from gout. He too looked backward, but to the days of Elizabeth, rather than to the Middle Ages. He wanted a return to harmony between King and Parliament, and argued that such harmony could again become possible only by giving the Crown the necessary authority and instruments to govern.

Wentworth's success in making Ireland financially self-supporting, so that no subsidies were required from England, made Charles eagerly follow his advice to call a new Parliament. But Wentworth's support at this juncture proved negligible. He had returned to England in poor health, suffering from dysentery as well as gout. And he found the country almost beyond help, thanks to Charles's habit of following the advice of such ministers as his comptroller Sir Henry Vane (father of the 1636–1637 governor of Massachusetts). Vane was more interested in flattering the King than in telling the hard truths of finance.

When Charles summoned Parliament after the longest "vacation" in its history, only one out of four members had served in the previous one of 1628–1629. And of the leaders of that Parliament, Sir John Eliot had rotted to death in prison, Sir

Edward Coke had died an old man of eighty-two in 1634, and Thomas Wentworth had gone over to the King's side. Only fifty-seven-year-old John Pym remained—Parliament's last, but also its best, hope for effective leadership. A scholarly appearing lawyer with a neatly pointed beard, he was from an ancient family, wealthy, and an alumnus of Oxford. He had already served in five Parliaments, two under King James, 1621 and 1624, and three under Charles, 1625, 1626, 1628–1629.

After the Commons Protestation of 1621—asserting Parliamentary involvement in the fields of foreign policy and church affairs, plus freedom of debate—Pym was put under house arrest. But he succeeded in avoiding further martyrdom, perhaps because his moderation was in distinct contrast to the fiery emotion of Eliot. Pym even decided to pay both the tax on ship money and the earlier forced loan, without protest.

During the eleven years of non-Parliamentary rule he had kept in constant touch with the Puritan opposition to Charles. He met regularly with such notables as Count Brooke, Viscount Saye and Sele, and the Earl of Warwick. All were members of the board directing settlement of Providence Island in the Caribbean—where they attempted unsuccessfully to establish their own outpost in competition with the Spanish—and the newly founded Connecticut colony. Used to working together on these colonial enterprises, these men formed a tight Puritan clique in Parliament.

As Parliament convened, April 13, 1640, Pym made a quiet-spoken, two-hour statement of grievances committed by the King "against the privileges and liberties of Parliament." He took as his theme: "A Parliament is that to the Commonwealth which the soul is to the body. . . . It behooves us therefore to keep the faculty of that soul from distempers." (He had moved Puritan religious theory of the supremacy of the soul in the body over into politics, where Parliament became supreme in the state.)

Under the leadership of Pym (nicknamed "King Pym"), Parliament held firmly to its ancient power of the purse, refusing to vote any taxes without concessions from the King to appease eleven years of pent-up grievances. A compromise appeared to be in the making as Wentworth advised the King to discontinue collections of ship money. But Wentworth was too sick to conduct the negotiations himself. And so the King delegated the task to the elder Sir Henry Vane. Vane botched any attempt at compromise. Either he was inept, or as some hinted, he acted on purpose to discredit Wentworth, his rival for the King's favor. Exactly three weeks after it was summoned, Parliament was abruptly adjourned.

Rioting broke out on the streets, and Wentworth recommended public torture and execution to discourage further outbursts. Two young rioters were caught and hanged publicly, one having the doubtful distinction of being the last person in English history to be tortured on the rack. Order was restored around London, but the Scottish rebels crossed the border and soon occupied northern areas of England. Desperate for money, his troops half-starved and mutinous, Charles arranged a humiliating two-month truce with the Scottish invaders and hastily called Parliament into session.

In the election campaign preceding the meeting of this Parliament, John Pym "rode about the country to promote the election of the puritanical brethren to serve in Parliament," in the words of contemporary diarist Anthony à Wood. At the same time, Wentworth, who despite his poor physical condition had been commanding the scraggly English army in the fight against the invading Scots, made his way south to lead the King's supporters in Parliament, commenting gloomily about his personal future: "I am tomorrow to London with

Vane, Father and Son, from 52 "playing card" cartoons of the Cromwell interregnum—Courtesy of the Trustees of the British Museum, London.

more danger beset, I believe, than ever man went out of Yorkshire." Rumors had reached him of mobs in the London streets, demonstrating for his death. Young Henry Vane, unsuccessful in his rebellion against his royalist father—and back in England for almost three years since his term as governor of Massachusetts Bay—handed over to Pym and the Puritans in Parliament records of the Privy Council meeting at which Strafford had suggested bringing in Irish troops to subdue England.

With the cross-hatching of plots and subplots, Parliament came into session, November 3, 1640. "A day never to be mentioned without a curse," snapped royalist John Evelyn in his diary. But a balladeer sang of popular expectations:

> Although this fair island abound with foul crimes
> The Parliament saith, we shall see better times.

"My Birds Have Flown"

"Reformation goes on . . . as hot as toast," a member of Parliament exulted in the summer of 1641. In less than a year, meeting from November 1640 to September 1641, with only occasional breaks lasting a few days, Parliament had changed the direction of English government.

Their very first concern was to get rid of the King's advisers. They blamed these men around the King, more than Charles himself, for the country's troubles. Under the leadership of John Pym—with the Scots now threatening to move on London and the King desperate for money—they attempted to impeach Archbishop Laud. When they could not prove the charge against him, they accomplished the same purpose by passing a bill of attainder. By the lopsided vote of 448 to 59, they sent him to the Tower where he was executed four years later. Chief Justice John Lord Finch, who had presided at the conviction of John Hampden for refusal to pay a ship-money levy, was driven out of England to exile in Holland.

Next, Parliament attempted to impeach Thomas Wentworth, the Earl of Strafford, and when that failed subjected him, too, to death by a bill of attainder. Oliver St. John, lawyer for John Hampden in the ship-money case, and now a member of Parliament, argued in favor of attainder and of dispensing with normal processes of the law, "for it was never accounted either cruelty or foul play to knock foxes or wolves on the heads . . . because they be beasts of prey."

The bill of attainder against the Earl of Strafford required, and finally received, the signature of King Charles, who first hesitated, then vacillated, and finally approved. John Evelyn described the execution in his diary:

On the twelfth of May, 1641, I beheld on Tower Hill the fatal stroke, which severed the wisest head in England from the shoulders of the Earl of Strafford, whose crime coming under the cognizance of no human law or statute, a new one was made, not to be a precedent, but his destruction. With what reluctancy the King signed the execution, he has sufficiently expressed; to which he imputes his own unjust suffering—to such exorbitancy were things arrived.

The execution of Strafford was by no means universally applauded. Poet Sir John Denham lamented:

Great Strafford! worthy of that name though all
Of thee could be forgotten, but thy fall,
Crushed by imaginary treason's weight,
Which too much merit did accumulate.

In a flood of activity, Parliament condemned taxes for ship money, exonerated John Hampden, canceled monopolies, and made Parliamentary control over tonnage and poundage absolute. The Star Chamber was abolished, and its most famous prisoners—Bastwick, Burton, and Lilburne—were released.

Never again would Parliament be dissolved against its will or not called into session for long periods of time. A Triennial Act was passed, insuring that Parliament would be called into session at least once every three years, and could be adjourned or dissolved only with their own consent, and after agreement by both the House of Lords and the House of Commons. (Compare the Massachusetts Bay Colony, where the General Court for elections by secret popular ballot was held yearly, in addition to at least three regular courts. Also compare the United States Constitution, Article I, Section 4: "The Congress shall assemble at least once in every year. . . ." Section 5: "Neither house, during the session of Congress, shall, without the consent of the other, adjourn for more than three days . . . .")

So far Lords and Commons had acted together in Parliament with near unanimity among themselves and with the general approval of the nation. They had even persuaded the financially desperate King to sign all legislation, although each act and bill further reduced his royal power.

Then rebellion erupted in Ireland. Native Catholics massacred hundreds, maybe thousands, of English Protestant soldiers and settlers.

The rebellion stemmed from the unfeeling policy of the recently executed Strafford, who had treated Ireland as his private preserve while serving as governor. But Parliament was certain that Queen Henrietta Maria had actively encouraged the massacre—which they quickly termed the "Queen's Rebellion." Everywhere they looked, they saw in the Irish action the fine Catholic hand of the still very un-English Henrietta Maria. They accused her of causing the rebellion, then convincing her husband to demand an army, supposedly to prevent further bloodshed, but actually to subvert the entire government of England. With an army at his disposal, the King would be able to force Parliament to follow his bidding, now that he could no longer use the threat of dissolution. In panic, both the House of Commons and the House of Lords insisted that any English troops raised to suppress the rebellion must be responsible to Parliament alone.

Reacting further to the Irish Rebellion, the Puritans in Commons pushed through a Grand Remonstrance to the King. With moderate John Pym in the lead, they cataloged everything that had gone wrong since Charles came to the throne, and reforms already passed by Parliament. Then, implying strongly that Parliament's contribution to the art of good government had become indispensable, they listed reforms still needed.

But the King's cause was far from hopeless. The well-entrenched tradition that the King was supreme, or at the very least was superior to Parliament, meant that Commons barely passed this Remonstrance by eleven votes, 159 to 148. And out of fear of rejection they never dared to ask the hidebound House of Lords for concurrence.

The struggle between King and Parliament remained a near draw in terms of national support, except for the almost unnoticed decision taken by a seemingly ordinary member of Commons. Rectangular-looking Oliver Cromwell—5-feet 10 inches tall, chunky build, early forties—finally cast aside all thought of migrating to the New World. He whispered in the ear of a fellow member of Parliament, Viscount Falkland, that with rejection of the Remonstrance, "he would have sold all he had the next morning and never seen England any more, and he knew there were many other honest men of the same resolution." Royalist Clarendon reporting Cromwell's remark in his near-contemporary *History of the Rebellion and Civil*

Wars, commented: "So near was the poor kingdom at that time to its deliverance."

Cromwell's role as the King's nemesis was for the future. At the moment it was the moderates who controlled Parliament. But such men as John Pym and John Hampden needed the cooperation of the King to keep England from falling into the abyss of civil war.

So far they had asked only to work with the King in order to return England to "ancient precedent." King Charles, however, rejected all efforts at compromise and conciliation. His highly emotional reaction to Commons' Grand Remonstrance was to ignore it totally, because he hated Pym for his role in the execution of Strafford.

Then on advice of his headstrong wife he resorted to what amounted to a *coup d'état*. He attempted to arrest five members of the House of Commons, including John Pym and John Hampden. Charles charged all five with attempting to "subvert the fundamental laws, with inviting the Scots to invade the kingdom of England, and raising tumults in order to compel Parliament to join them in their treacherous designs." For good measure he also ordered the arrest of Lord Mandeville, son of the Earl of Manchester, and a leading Puritan rebel in the House of Lords.

For hundreds of years the House of Lords had had the sole prerogative to arrest members of Parliament. Now the House of Lords angrily refused the King's demand to order the arrest of Lord Mandeville and the five members of Commons. So the King himself went to Commons to press his charges and have the five men arrested. With great good manners he asked permission to sit in the Speaker's chair, greeted those members whose names or faces he found familiar, and then asked the five members to step forward.

Stunned silence followed. The King looked to House

Oliver Cromwell, by Robert Walker, ca. 1649—Courtesy National
Portrait Gallery, London.

Lenthall runs away With his Mace to the Army.

Lenthall with mace, the symbol of authority. From 52 "playing cards" cartoons of the Cromwell interregnum—Courtesy of the Trustees of the British Museum, London.

Speaker William Lenthall, fifty-year-old Oxford barrister, wealthy, and new at his job. Falling to his knees immediately, but spurning the Speaker's traditional role of royal mouthpiece, Lenthall declared: "Sire, I have neither eyes to see nor tongue to speak in this place but as the House is pleased to direct me."

The King turned to John Pym's customary seat, and finding it empty, turned to the others, also empty. He rebuked and threatened Commons: "Since I see all my birds have flown, I do expect that you will send them unto me as soon as they return hither."

Well warned before the King's appearance on the floor of Commons, the five leaders had fled out of his reach to the protection of the thoroughly Puritan London Common Council. "Privileges of Parliament, Privileges of Parliament," the

Council responded to the King's demand that they hand over the fugitives, January 3, 1642.

The King took no prisoners, but his action forced Pym into a more radical position. Clarendon later wrote about Pym in his *History:* "From the time of his being accused of high treason by the King . . . he never entertained thoughts of moderation, but always opposed all overtures of peace and accommodation."

In his blunderheaded attempt to overthrow Parliament's leadership by force, Charles's defiance of the House of Lords nudged the Upper House back into close alliance with Commons. By February 1642, the House of Lords finally assented to legislation long advocated by Commons, exclusion from membership in the Upper House of Anglican bishops who could be counted on for unwavering support of the King even in matters of Parliamentary prerogative.

The following month, March 1642, Lords and Commons banded together against the King to pass the Militia Bill, looking to the use of force against the still smoldering Irish rebellion, but with control firmly in the hands of Parliament. The King, who up till now had signed even legislation he found personally distasteful or humiliating, flatly refused to give up control of the armed forces. For the first time since the convening of this Parliament, Charles withheld his signature to duly passed legislation.

Posthaste, Pym and Parliament gave the King their ultimatum: the Nineteen Propositions. Permanent Parliamentary supremacy must be acknowledged, and the King reduced to a weak constitutional monarch (as Queen Elizabeth II is today). Completely rejecting the Propositions, the King stormed: "These being passed, we may be waited on bareheaded, we may have our hand kissed, the style of Majesty continued to us, and the King's authority declared by both Houses of Parliament may be still the style of your commands. . . . But as to time and real power we should remain but the outside, but the picture, but the sign of a King." Two months later the King raised his standard at Nottingham. The Civil War was on.

The country cracked into two gigantic forces. The House of Commons supplied 302 members to the Puritan antiroyalist banner, demanding Parliamentary supremacy over the King. The royalists won some 236 adherents from the same House of Commons (and a few took no position at all). In the House of Lords, the Puritans attracted about 30 peers to their side, while the King had the support of about 60 others. The remaining 30 or so members of the Upper House were too old, too sick, or were just plain sitting the Civil War out by staying abroad. Citizens from the rural, less industrialized north and west sections of England tended to side with the King, while those from the highly commercialized south and east, and the large cities and ports, tended to join the Puritans.

As in all civil wars, families divided on opposite sides. And the great mass of people, those living at or below subsistence level, took no side at all. In fact, at one point during a major battle, an advance patrol warned a farm laborer to get out of the way to avoid injury in the fighting between King and Parliament. "What! Has them two fallen out then!" he exclaimed.

By mid-1643, a year after the start of the Civil War, Parliament had lost its two top leaders. John Pym, the man most responsible for its recent achievements and contributions to constitutionalism, was dying of cancer. And his second in command, John Hampden, had left Parliament for the battlefield where he was mortally wounded on June 18, 1643, and died one week later. Henry Vane the Younger, who had served as Governor of Massachusetts Bay 1636–1637 during the controversy over Anne Hutchinson, succeeded Pym as leader of Parliament.

On June 14, 1643, Parliament took a giant step backward.
It ordered licensing of the press—meaning no license for pub-
lications that criticized Parliament, or otherwise merited its
disapproval. This was uncomfortably close to the censorship
that had been practiced by the hated and now abolished Star
Chamber.

In horror at Parliament's baring its tyrannical teeth, England's literary giant, Puritan John Milton, protested shortly
afterward: "Give me the liberty to know, to utter, and to argue freely according to conscience above all liberties." In
Areopagitica, Milton—whose fame rests on his poetry, but
who is most widely quoted as the political theorist and conscience of Puritanism—continued: "Though all the winds of
doctrine were let loose to play upon the earth, so Truth be in
the field, we do injuriously by licensing and prohibiting to

misdoubt her strength. Let her and Falsehood grapple; who ever knew Truth put to the worse, in a free and open encounter." (Milton's seventeenth-century essay, the starting point and final word for any discussion of freedom of speech and of press, was recently quoted by James Reston in a *New York Times* column defending the *Times'* release of the Pentagon Papers in the spring of 1971.)

The blood-flowing years of the Civil War lasted until 1649. At first the royalists (cavaliers), quite used to horseback riding as one of their constant gentlemanly pursuits, did quite well on the basis of excellent cavalry. But when Oliver Cromwell entered the picture—with a strong sense of organization and innovation, and a fierce temper—he forged the Parliamentary army into the tightly disciplined and famous Ironsides. He staffed his army with political and religious radicals, sneeringly dubbed *roundheads* because of their short haircuts by the long-haired members of the upper class. Reorganized as the New Model Army, the Cromwellians won a crucial battle at Marston Moor, 1644, and a year later trounced Charles completely at Naseby. In desperation Charles fled to the Scots, of all people. The Scots had been prevailed upon to defend the Scottish-born King who was, they were told as they received promises of money, defending all of Britain against the radicalism of the English Puritan Parliament. But when the money failed to come through as promised, the Scots turned the King over to Parliament in return for back pay amounting to £400,000.

As the war continued, extremists seized control of the army, captured Charles and demanded that he be dethroned. Roundhead leaders authorized Colonel Thomas Pride, who in civilian life had hauled goods for a living, to purge Parliament, leaving behind only the radicals. English history can be marvelously descriptive in its use of names. Pride's Purge left

Pride, Oliver's Drayman, from 52 "playing cards" cartoons of the Cromwell Interregnum—Courtesy of the Trustees of the British Museum, London.

behind a Rump Parliament consisting of only 60 radicals or roundheads out of the full Commons membership of more than 500 men.

Striking with tornadolike speed, the Rump brought King Charles to trial for his life before a carefully preselected court of radicals, and sentenced him to die three days later on January 30, 1649. Their haste resulted partly from their unprovable theory that the end of Europe's Thirty Years' War in 1648 left countless German soldiers with nothing better to do than invade the British Isles at Ireland, the weakest point, and attempt to restore Charles to full power.

France in 1793 and Russia in 1918 each killed their monarch amidst revolutionary turmoil. But only England acted with baroque splendor. Charles I was made to walk to his death through the 110-foot hall of the Banqueting House, designed in 1620 by England's first great architect, Inigo Jones. High above the King's head were the huge ceiling panels he himself had commissioned Peter Paul Rubens to paint, glorifying the wise rule of Charles's father, James I, and the blessings of divine right monarchy. The executioner's block stood just a few yards outside.

In the most frequently quoted poem written on the King's execution, Andrew Marvell, still in his twenties, described Charles's martyrdom:

> He nothing common did or mean
> Upon that memorable scene;
> But with his keener eye
> The axe's edge did try:
> Nor called the gods with vulgar spite
> To vindicate his helpless right,
> But bowed his comely head
> Down as upon a bed.

Royalist John Evelyn mourned in his diary: "The villainy of the rebels proceeding now so far as to try, condemn, and murder our excellent King on the 30th of this month, struck me with such sorrow, that I kept the day of his martyrdom a fast, and would not be present."

In contrast, Puritan John Milton, writing on the execution of King Charles in 1649—*The Tenure of Kings and Magistrates*—took as his theme: "That it is lawful and hath been held so through all ages, for any, who had the power, to call to account a tyrant, or wicked king, and after due conviction, to depose, and put him to death."

In words that express the tie between the English Revolution of 1640–1660, and the American Declaration of Independence of 1776, he wrote:

Bradshaw in ye High Court of
Justice insulting of the King.

Bradshaw in the High Court
of Justice insulting the King.

The High Court of Justice or
Olivers slaughter house.

The High Court of Injustice
or Oliver's Slaughterhouse.

The Rump and dreggs of the house
of Com: remaining after the good
members were purged out.

The Rump and the dregs
of the House of Commons after
the good members were purged out.

The Rump roasted salt it well
it stinks exceedingly.

The Rump roasted—salt it well,
it stinks exceedingly. All from 52
"playing cards" cartoons of the
Cromwell Interregnum—Courtesy
of the Trustees of the British
Museum, London.

Bradshaw the Jailer and the Hangman, Keepers of the Liberty of England, from 52 "playing cards" cartoons of the Cromwell Interregnum—Courtesy of the Trustees of the British Museum, London.

While as the magistrate was set above the people, so the law was set above the magistrate . . . with the express warning that if the king or magistrate proved unfaithful to his trust, the people would be disengaged. . . . It follows that since the King or magistrate holds his authority of the people, both originally and naturally for their own good in the first place, and not his own, then may the people as oft as they shall judge it for the best, either choose him or reject him, retain him or depose him though no tyrant, merely by the liberty and right of free-born men, to be governed as seems to them best. . . .

The power of Kings and magistrates . . . was and is originally the people's and by them conferred in trust only to be employed to the common peace and benefit; with liberty therefore and right remaining in them to re-

Oliver Seeking God While the King is Murdered by his Order, from 52 "playing cards" cartoons of the Cromwell interregnum—Courtesy of the Trustees of the British Museum, London.

assume it to themselves, if by Kings or magistrates it be abused; or to dispose of it by any alteration, as they shall judge most conducting to the public good.

Similar Puritan political thought had already been expressed in the New World. In 1776 it would again crop up in the opening paragraphs of the Declaration of Independence: "Governments are instituted among men, deriving their just powers from the consent of the governed; . . . whenever any form of government becomes destructive of these ends, it is the right of the people to alter or abolish it and so institute new government, laying its foundation on such principles and organizing its powers in such form, as to them shall seem most likely to effect their safety and happiness."

However, most of England mourned the King's death.

Even Oliver Cromwell, according to a legend handed down by contemporary writers, went by himself at night to visit the body of the murdered monarch at Whitehall Palace. Supposedly, Cromwell lifted the lid of the coffin, stared at the face in silence, and after a long time muttered, "Cruel necessity." The legend may be no more true than the story of George Washington and the cherry tree, although there is evidence that Cromwell was one of the last to assent to the King's death. After the execution, though, Cromwell persuaded himself that England had rid herself of tyranny "in a way which Christians in after times will mention with honor, and all tyrants in the world will look at with fear."

England, which had 'always doted on precedent and tradition, was off to a rocky start as a republic or commonwealth. On the other side of the Atlantic, New England, which had prospered in the 1630s while England persecuted, found itself in the 1640s no longer needed as an escape hatch.

To the surprise of no one, but to the dismay of many New Englanders, emigration to the New World halted almost completely, with the avalanche of radical changes instituted by Parliament. By June 1641, John Winthrop bewailed in his journal: "The Parliament of England setting upon a general reformation both of church and state, the Earl of Strafford being beheaded, and the Archbishop Laud (our great enemy) and many others of the great officers and judges, bishops, and others, imprisoned and called to account, this caused all men to stay in England in expectation of a new world, so as few coming to us, all foreign commodities grew scarce, and our own of no price."

In the future New England could go in any one of three directions. It could become defensively and economically self-sufficient . . . or draw closer to England . . . or admit complete failure.

"Wild Beasts and Beastlike Men"

Like most New Englanders, Anne Bradstreet greeted news of
Mother England's cataclysm with a mixture of sympathy and
superiority. In a house full of politics and children—she was
daughter of one permanent magistrate, Thomas Dudley, and
wife of another, Simon Bradstreet—this thirty-year-old
mother of eight invented the rhymed "Dialogue between Old
England and New":

New England

Alas dear Mother, fairest Queen and best
With honour, wealth, and peace, happy and blest;
What ails thee hang thy head, and cross thine arms?
And sit i'th' dust, to sigh these sad alarms?
What deluge of new woes thus over-whelm
The glories of thy ever famous Realm?
What means this wailing tone, this mournful guise?
Ah, tell thy daughter, she may sympathize.

England [at the end of a long threnody of complaint
and woe]

. . . .

Well to the matter then, there's grown of late
Twixt King and Peers a question of state:
Which is the chief, the law, or else the King?
One said, it's he, the other no such thing.
'Tis said, my better part in Parliament
To ease my groaning Land, showed their intent,
To crush the proud, and right to each man deal,
To help the Church, and stay the common-weal.

. . . .

Old customs, new prerogative stood on,
Had they not held Law fast, all had been gone.

. . . .

But these may be beginnings of more woe
Who knows, but this may be my overthrow.
Oh pity me in this sad perturbation
My plundered towns, my houses devastation.

. . . .

Abruptly, the great New England migration began re-
versing itself, with hundreds of colonists departing to throw
their minds and bodies on the side of Parliament. Prominent
returnees included John Winthrop's young son Stephen, born
1619, who became a major-general in the Parliamentary
army; Israel Stoughton, a Massachusetts assistant and leader in
the Pequot War, and George Fenwick, a founder of Connecticut, both of whom commanded Parliamentary regi-
ments; John Leverett, later governor of Massachusetts, who

served as aide to Parliamentary commander Oliver Cromwell; George Downing, young nephew of John Winthrop and member of Harvard's first graduating class, who in the 1650s, with Parliament and Cromwell in command of England, served as intelligence officer of the English army in Scotland, ambassador to the Netherlands, and member of Parliament (and bequeathed his name to Downing Street, upon which the modern prime minister of England lives, at Number Ten).

Another New Englander joining the struggle against King Charles was Edward Hopkins, Governor of Connecticut, who was elected to Parliament and who served at various times as Warden for the Fleet, and as Commissioner for the Navy and Admiralty. In his case, the decision to abandon the New World may have stemmed equally from his political dedication and from his wife's complete mental breakdown after years of wilderness living.

With more antifeminism than sympathy for this gifted woman, John Winthrop had spewed out an absolute diatribe against her in his journal after their first meeting:

Mr. Hopkins, the Governor of Hartford upon Connecticut, came to Boston, and brought his wife with him (a godly young woman, and of special parts,) who was fallen into a sad infirmity, the loss of her understanding and reason, which had been growing upon her divers years, by occasion of her giving herself wholly to reading and writing, and had written many books. Her husband, being very loving and tender of her, was loath to grieve her; but he saw his error, when it was too late. For if she had attended her household affairs, and such things as belong to women, and not gone out of her way and calling to meddle in such things as are proper for men whose minds are stronger, etc., she had kept her wits, and might have improved them usefully and honorably in the place God had set her. He brought her to Boston, and left her with her brother, one Mr. Yale, a merchant, to try what means might be had there for her. But no help could be had.

(Elihu Yale, founder of Yale University, was the nephew of Mrs. Hopkins.)

Not only George Downing, but six others of the nine members of Harvard's first graduating class of 1641 were among the returnees. And over the next five years, a heavy majority of Harvard graduates participated in the ongoing English Civil War, until by 1646, Massachusetts, Plymouth, Connecticut, and New Haven issued a joint declaration that they "thought fit that some course be taken with the parents and with such scholars themselves (as the case may require) that when they are furnished with learning, in some competent measure, they remove not into other countries, but improve their parts and abilities for the service of the colonies."

Yet Massachusetts itself had contributed to this well-educated exodus. The General Court sent two prominent and fearlessly articulate ministers, Thomas Welde of Roxbury and Hugh Peter of Salem, as representatives of the Commonwealth to show support for Parliament. Both graduates of Trinity College, Cambridge, and both members of Harvard's first board of overseers, where they had played great roles in the founding of Harvard College, they had each made unique contributions to the Bay Colony in their few years' residence. Hugh Peter found a profitable market for dried codfish, which rapidly became one of the basic sources of income for Massachusetts. And Thomas Welde co-authored the *Bay Psalm Book*.

John Winthrop, Jr., married to the stepdaughter of Hugh

Peter, also went along on the mission to England, described by John Winthrop, Sr.: "They [the General Court] thought fit to send some chosen men into England to congratulate the happy success there and to satisfy our creditors of the true cause why we could not make so current payment now as in former years we had done, and to be ready to make use of any opportunity God should offer for the good of the country here, as also to give any advice, as it should be required, for the settling of the right form of church discipline there. . . ."

Peter and Welde decided to remain permanently in England, but John Winthrop, Jr., made several trips back and forth, attempting to restore the economic credit of the colony and to obtain additional loans. With the initial success of the Long Parliament, he had somehow to convince wealthy Puritans such as Lord Saye to continue lending and sending money, even though they no longer needed to reserve a refuge for themselves in the New World.

The shriveling of loans and gifts occurred simultaneously with the decrease of shipping to New England, the result of the English Civil War. This meant few imports of food and supplies from England, and the marked reduction of new arrivals who needed to purchase local agricultural products or to hire labor for housing. An unknown Puritan lamented:

> Men no more the Sea pass o'er, and
> Customers are wanting.

And by September 1642, John Winthrop was bemoaning to his private journal: "The sudden fall of land and cattle, and the scarcity of foreign commodities, and money, etc., with the thin access of people from England, put many into an unsettled frame of spirit, so as they concluded there would be no subsisting here, and accordingly they began to hasten away."

However, John Winthrop stubbornly determined not "to hasten away." All over again he appeased his conscience for abandoning his family's ancient homeland. His old friend and neighbor in Suffolk County, England, Sir Nathaniel Barnardiston, again a member of Parliament, wrote pleadingly: "Now we see and feel how much we are weakened by the loss of those that are gone from us, who should have stood in the gap, and have wrought and wrestled mightily in this great business."

Governor Winthrop recorded his answering thoughts in the privacy of his journal:

For such as come together into a wilderness, where are nothing but wild beasts and beastlike men, and there confederate together in civil and church estate, whereby they do, implicitly at least, bind themselves to support each other, and all of them that society, whether civil or sacred, whereof they are members, how they can break from this without free consent, is hard to find, so as may satisfy a tender or good conscience in time of trial. Ask thy conscience, if thou wouldst have plucked up thy stakes, and brought thy family 3,000 miles, if thou hadst expected that all, or most, would have forsaken thee there. . . . If one may go, another may, and so the greater part, and so church and commonwealth may be left destitute in a wilderness, exposed to misery and reproach, and all for their ease and pleasure.

Like John Winthrop most of the Bay settlers had become more American than English. Proudly looking around, they saw that the near-flood of revolutionary political actions Massachusetts Bay had put into effect the first six years of settlement had been imitated by their sister colonies, Plymouth and Connecticut. In 1636, Plymouth drew up its own Great Fundamentals, the first written code of politics in America, including in nine paragraphs the essence of the Bay Colony government: annual meetings in which the Plymouth freemen would elect their governor, deputy governor, and assistants; laws would be enacted by an assembly or general court, consisting of two representatives from each town chosen by local freemen, plus the governor and his assistants. In 1639, Connecticut adopted the Fundamental Orders, likewise establishing a framework of government similar to that of Massachusetts.

Plymouth and Connecticut had imitated the ideas of Massachusetts. Now Massachusetts wanted to go even further by committing its government, and all of the laws and liberties under it, to writing. That way, everybody could see and know their rights and duties. Otherwise, thirteen magistrates—governor, deputy governor, and eleven assistants—might take it into their heads to behave like a King and Privy Council.

Theoretically, subjecting the magistrates to yearly election by the freemen, and to meetings in the General Court with the more popularly representative town deputies, should insure against arbitrary government. But in practice, what started out as a benign aristocracy frightened many with signs that it could easily rot into a malignant oligarchy.

In the eleven Bay Company elections, 1630–1640, a total of only 26 names had appeared on the list of magistrates chosen yearly, whereas 143 magisterial positions—at the rate of 13 per year—were supposedly available. Worse yet from the viewpoint of the worriers, even fewer than these 26 men—11 to be exact—were on the rolls as having served for periods ranging from four to eleven years.

John Winthrop and Thomas Dudley served every single year either as governor, deputy governor, or assistant. Simon

Simon Bradstreet—From the Massachusetts State House Collection.
Courtesy of the Secretary of the Commonwealth of Massachusetts.
Photo by the author.

Bradstreet, Dudley's son-in-law, was an assistant from the very
beginning, as was Increase Nowell, the man who gave up his
position as Church Elder for election to the civil government.
Also serving for long periods was old John Endecott who
was elected assistant eight times, with the conspicuous exception of the year he was purposely excluded as punishment for
removing the cross from the royal flag.

Elections might be one way to prevent despotism, but the
time had come to institute a government of written laws to
restrain those who were elected. Massachusetts hoped to im-

prove on Plymouth's Great Fundamentals and Connecticut's Fundamental Orders, and could hardly help noticing that the smaller colonies had never suffered royal retaliation by having their governments in writing.

When Plymouth wrote its political code in 1636, the King was harassed but very much in charge of England. Similarly, when Connecticut produced its framework of government in 1639, the King was embroiled in war with Scotland but still getting along quite well without Parliament. But by 1641, at the time of the annual Bay election, the King was facing a strong Parliamentary challenge and was directly threatened by Scottish invaders on English soil. Certainly if he had not bothered the Englishmen of Plymouth or of Connecticut in the 1630s, he had less power, and probably less inclination, to threaten the Englishmen of Massachusetts in 1641. A written code of laws, even if it contained provisions contrary to the royal interpretation of English laws, no longer portended instant recall of the Massachusetts Charter—the bogey John Winthrop had successfully raised every year since at least 1636.

The whole situation had changed. But not so the minds of John Winthrop and his like-minded allies in the magistracy. They continued to press for government by unwritten—and hence flexible—precedent, until someday in the far-off future when the colony would have more stability and experience. They lost their argument, however, in the annual election of 1641, after which John Winthrop recorded in his diary, with an admirable lack of emotion and an annoying lack of detail: "There had been much laboring to have Mr. Bellingham chosen [governor] and when the votes were numbered he had six more than the others."

With Winthrop out and Parliament in, the Massachusetts General Court passed the Massachusetts Body of Liberties at its November 1641 session. Ironically, there is no record of the proceedings except for the journal of John Winthrop, then serving as assistant: "This session continued three weeks, and established 100 laws, which were called the *Body of Liberties.* They had been composed by Mr. Nathaniel Ward (sometime pastor of the church of Ipswich; he had been a minister in England, and formerly a student and practiser in the course of the common law,) and had been revised and altered by the court, and sent forth into every town to be further considered of, and now again in this court, they were revised, amended, and presented, and so established for three years, by that experience to have them fully amended and established to be perpetual."

Sixty-two-year-old Nathaniel Ward, author of the Body of Liberties, was a graduate of Emmanuel College, Cambridge. Ward's long periods practicing law and preaching in the ministry reflected his prime goals in life—the prevention of arbitrary government and the establishment of strict discipline. He was a dour intellectual who occasionally erupted into humor at the expense of his pet prejudices, against allowing religious toleration and against women. His 1647 book *The Simple Cobbler of Aggawam,* published after he retired to England to live out his final years, is filled with wittiness, both clever and perverse. This rhyme on women, for example:

> The world is full of care,
> Much like unto a bubble;
> Women and care, and care and women,
> And women and care and trouble.

Yet, another of his rhymes reveals him as attached to orderly procedure through words:

The world's a well strung fiddle, man's tongue the
    quill,
That fills the world with fumble for want of skill,
When things and words in tune and tone do meet,
The universal song goes smooth and sweet.

Ward drafted the Massachusetts Body of Liberties, proceeding from the assumption that the people "may not be denied their proper and lawful liberties." Then, as Winthrop
noted, the General Court put the code of laws into final form.

The very first clause of the Body of Liberties assured a government of laws not men, established to protect life, liberty,
and property:

No man's life shall be taken away, no man's honour or
good name shall be stained, no man's person shall be arrested, restrained, banished, dismembered, nor any way
punished; no man shall be deprived of his wife or children, no man's goods or estate shall be taken away from
him, nor any way damaged under colour of law or coun-
tenance of authority, unless it be by virtue or equity of
some express law of the country warranting the same, established by a general court and sufficiently published, or
in case of the defect of a law in any particular case by the
word of God. And in capital cases, or in cases concerning
dismembering or banishment, according to that word to
be judged by the General Court.

(By 1776 these ideas were so well known and universally accepted in the thirteen colonies that they could be embraced in
a few words: "life, liberty, and the pursuit of happiness," in
the opening paragraph of the Declaration of Independence.)

Clause 7 defined the war-making power as held "by the counsel and consent of a Court General, or by Authority derived from the same." (Compare United States Constitution—advice and consent of United States Senate on treaties, and declaration of war by Congress.)

Harking back to the royal abuse of monopolies in England, so frequently the subject of Parliamentary attention under James and Charles, Clause 9 asserted: "No monopolies shall be granted or allowed amongst us, but of such new inventions that are profitable to the country, and that for a short time." (Compare the United States Constitution, Article I, Section 8: "Congress shall have the power . . . to promote the progress of science and useful arts, by securing for limited times to authors and inventors the exclusive right to their respective writings and discoveries.")

According to Clause 12, every man in the colony, "whether inhabitant or foreigner," freeman or not, was granted liberty "to attend all public meetings and to make motions and debate all questions." Allowing all Massachusetts men to initiate legislation gave them a privilege extended in the rest of the world only to heads of state, the clergy, or, as in England, to a select few.

Clause 17 permitted men to leave the colony at will, a radical notion in the seventeenth century when their own English King controlled emigration abroad, or movement from one county to the next. In the twentieth century, the concept of freedom of movement and travel has still failed to achieve universal acceptance.

Remembering the treatment of Darnel and the five knights who, refusing to pay the forced loan of 1626, were arbitrarily thrown into prison and denied the right of bail, Clause 18 read: "No man's person shall be restrained or imprisoned by any authority whatsoever, before the law hath sentenced him thereto, if he can put in sufficient security or bail . . . for his appearance and good behavior in the mean time. . . ." (United States Constitution, Article I, Section 9: "The privilege of the writ of *habeas corpus* shall not be suspended"; Amendment V: "No person shall be held to answer for a capital or other infamous crime unless on a presentment or indictment of a grand jury"; Amendment VI: "In all criminal prosecutions, the accused shall enjoy the right to a speedy and public trial . . . and to be informed of the nature and cause of the accusation.")

Double jeopardy was outlawed in Clause 42: "No man shall be twice sentenced by civil justice for one and the same crime, offense, or trespass. (Compare, United States Constitution, Amendment V: "Nor shall any person be subject for the same offense to be twice put in jeopardy of life or limb. . . .")

Other liberties taken for granted by seventeenth-century Englishmen and considered as American today as Thanksgiving and the Fourth of July were carefully spelled out in the Body of Liberties and freely borrowed 150 years later by the infant United States. Massachusetts Clause 45: "No man shall be forced by torture to confess any crime against himself. (United States Constitution, Amendment V: "No person . . . shall be compelled in any criminal case to be a witness against himself. . . .") Massachusetts Clause 46: "For bodily punishments we allow amongst us none that are inhumane, barbarous, or cruel." (United States Constitution, Amendment VIII reads in part "nor cruel and unusual punishments inflicted.")

The United States voting age, recently lowered from twenty-one to eighteen, was set at twenty-one in Clause 53: "The age of discretion for passing away of lands or such kinds of herediments, or for giving of votes, verdicts, or sentence in any civil courts or causes, shall be one and twenty years."

Initiating the tradition of a written—as opposed to a conventional word-of-mouth—constitution, the Body of Liberties detailed the workings of the eleven-year-old Massachusetts self-government, and included a code of laws and bill of rights. Looking back to England, where only the need for more funds to fight the war against Scotland had brought Parliament back into existence, Massachusetts distinctly stated in Clause 67: "It is the constant liberty of the free men of this plantation to choose yearly at the Court of Election out of the freemen all the general officers of this jurisdiction. If they please to discharge them at the day of election by way of vote, they may do it without showing cause. But if at any other general court, we hold it due justice that the reasons thereof be alleged and proved. . . ." The rulers would not be allowed to rule arbitrarily, but neither would citizens have the right to throw out their rulers at any old time on an impulsive whim. Again looking at England, specifically the recently passed Triennial Act in the Long Parliament, Clause 69 read: "No general court shall be dissolved or adjourned without the consent of the major part thereof."

King Charles had indelibly impressed on Massachusetts Puritans his ability to martyr their leaders for attempting to speak freely in Parliamentary debate. The King's imprisonment of Parliamentary leaders and his final dissolution of Parliament in 1629 had preceded by a matter of exactly five months the fateful decision of some 1,000 Puritans to embark for New England, carrying independence with them in the form of the Charter of 1629, which specified no place of annual meeting or royal supervision.

Now in three different clauses they detailed freedom of speech and freedom of debate. Clause 70: "All freemen called to give any advice, vote, verdict, or sentence in any court, council, or civil assembly, shall have full freedom to do it according to their true judgments and consciences, so it be done orderly and inoffensively for the manner." Clause 75 further affirmed freedom of debate: "It is and shall be the liberty of any member or members of any court, council, or civil assembly in cases of making or executing any order or law, that properly concern religion, or any cause capital, or wars, or subscription to any public articles or remonstrance, in case they cannot in judgment and conscience consent to that way the major vote or suffrage goes, to make their *contra* remonstrance or protestation in speech or writing, and upon request to have their dissent recorded in the rolls of that court, so it be done Christianly and respectively for the manner." The clause concludes with a jolt to those who picture Puritans sitting uncomplainingly on hard benches: "And their dissent only be entered without the reasons thereof, for the avoiding of tediousness."

Clause 77 confers the precious right to keep silent: "In all cases wherein any freeman is to give his vote, be it in point of election, making constitutions and orders, or passing sentence in any case of judicature or the like, if he cannot see reason to give it positively one way or another, he shall have liberty to be silent, and not [be] pressed to a determined vote."

"Liberties of Women" are the subject of two clauses. According to Clause 79, a man must provide for support of his wife after his own death by leaving "a competent portion of his estate." If he fails to do this, the wife or widow may look to the General Court for relief. And contrary to the practice in England where wife-beating was permitted by common law, Clause 80 reads that unless the woman has assaulted her husband first, "every married woman shall be free from bodily correction or stripes by her husband."

In 1886, the Statue of Liberty was dedicated in New York harbor, with an inscription written by Emma Lazarus and reading in part:

> Give me your tired, your poor,
> Your huddled masses yearning to breathe free,
> The wretched refuse of your teeming shore,
> Send these, the homeless, tempest-tossed, to me:
> I lift my lamp beside the golden door.

Included in the Massachusetts Body of Liberties was the following, Clause 89: "If any people of other nations professing the true Christian religion shall flee to us from the tyranny or oppression of their persecutors, or from famine, wars, or the like necessary and compulsory cause, they shall be entertained and succoured amongst us, according to that power and prudence God shall give us."

All these prescriptions and promises of 1641 formed a strong foundation for the future of Massachusetts and United States law. But at the time of enactment, objections were immediately raised that there were too many omissions of orders and acts already established in the colony. Too many generalities was another reason for protest. Two problems remained —the so-called negative voice, and the amount of discretion to be left to the magistrates.

The "negative voice" had festered as an increasingly sore point between supporters and opponents of John Winthrop's philosophy of government. To John Winthrop, only a few men possessed the necessary qualifications for governing. They were truly aristocrats, not in the sense of possessing money or land, but because of their superior intelligence and sense of obligation to use their God-given abilities for the greatest good of the community, the Puritan ideal of following one's calling.

Winthrop had been decidedly uncomfortable with the admission of deputies representing the towns to the General Court (the result of the Watertown Protest of 1632). Since the General Court handled administrative as well as judicial powers, these men—good, true, but unlearned—had power equal to the relatively few supreme intellectuals of the Commonwealth. Winthrop's solution had been to persuade the General Court to grant the veto power of a negative voice to each of the two groups in the General Court, the magistrates and the deputies.

Eventually, however, the negative voice caused a wide division between magistrates and deputies, resulting in deadlocked General Court sessions. It took a stray sow, a poor but stubborn woman whose husband had left her alone in the wilds of New England while he was in England, and a wealthy man unpopular for his harsh dealings as a moneylender, to force a solution.

"*A Little Speech*"

"There fell out a great business on a very small occasion," John Winthrop disclosed in June 1642. Captain Robert Keayne, wealthy Boston merchant "of ill report in the country"—and censured many times both by Church and court for merciless treatment of those who owed him money—kept as his own a stray sow, which had been found wandering around town.

Keayne would have been the classic villain, except that he took the trouble to advertise the stray in hopes that the true owner would take it away. For a year no one did. Then Elizabeth Sherman, a poor woman, all alone and having to fend for herself in the temporary absence of her husband, sued Captain Keayne. The sow was her own lost property, she claimed. But with no settled court procedure for hearing lawsuits, the case bounced about, heard first as a matter of Church discipline by the Elders of the First Church of Boston, who decided in Keayne's favor "upon hearing all allegations and the most material witnesses on both parts."

Not at all satisfied, Goody Sherman took her case to the inferior court at Boston. Again she lost, and Keayne took revenge. He sued her for slander and won £20 from the jury. Furious at Keayne, the court, and the jury, and goaded by popular support for her cause, Elizabeth Sherman appealed to the General Court. For seven days the court listened to both sides of the question: "Whether the defendant be found to have been possessed of the plaintiff's sow and converted her to his own use or not." John Winthrop confided to his journal: "Much contention and earnestness there was, which indeed did mostly arise from the difficulty of the case, in regard of the cross witnesses, and some prejudices (as one professed) against the person, which blinded some men's judgments that they could not attend the true nature and course of the evidence."

The vote in the General Court was two magistrates and fifteen deputies in favor of Elizabeth Sherman, and seven magistrates and eight deputies for Robert Keayne, with seven abstaining. Counting all votes together, Goody Sherman would have won, seventeen to fifteen. But the law required that a majority of the magistrates and a majority of the deputies should agree on any verdict. And in the case at hand, a majority of the town deputies supported Goody Sherman, whereas almost all the aristocratically inclined magistrates favored Captain Keayne.

Stalemate followed, broken finally by a decision against Elizabeth Sherman and in favor of Robert Keayne. Winthrop noted dismally: Many spoke "unreverently of the court, especially of the Magistrates, and the report went out that their negative voice had hindered the course of justice."

This was the end of the litigation, but negative voice ballooned into major controversy dividing the colony. The power of the magistrates versus the will of the people was at stake.

John Winthrop bore down hard on retaining final power for a tiny minority of well-informed, well-intentioned men, the Magistracy. The veto power of the magistrates had been in use for ten years, since 1634, he insisted, conformed well to the Puritan ideal of calling, and could be justified on the basis of the wording of the original charter. But all the deputies, plus the same two magistrates, Richard Saltonstall, Jr., and Richard Bellingham, who had voted in favor of giving the sow to Elizabeth Sherman, clamored for more power.

At the March 1644 session of the General Court, the power of the magistrates to veto the actions of the deputies was diluted by compromise. Future disagreements between the duly "called" magistrates and the town deputies—"democratical" was Winthrop's epithet for them—would be fought out not in a single legislative chamber, but two. There would be the Magistracy and the House of Deputies. The Court itself carefully explained the reasons, and then detailed the working of the new arrangement:

> It is ordered, first that the Magistrates may sit and act business by themselves, by drawing up bills and orders, which they shall see good in their wisdom, which having agreed upon, they may present them to the Deputies to be considered of, how good and wholesome such orders are for the country, and accordingly to give their assent or dissent; the Deputies in like manner sitting apart by themselves, and consulting about such orders and laws as they in their discretion and experience shall find meet for common good, which, agreed upon by them, they may present to the Magistrates, who according to their wisdom having seriously considered of them, may consent unto them or disallow them; and when any orders

have passed the approbation of both Magistrates and Deputies, then such orders to be engrossed, and in the last day of the Court, to be read deliberately, and full assent to be given; provided also, that all matters of judicature, which this Court shall take cognizance of, shall be issued in like manner.

This establishment of a bicameral legislature climaxed fourteen years of Puritan political creativity. Massachusetts had now put the finishing touches on its government for the next forty years—long enough to deluge the future with political theories that actually worked.

The new bicameral legislature in Massachusetts diminished the power of the magistrates, and at the same time reduced the authority of the Church. The very act of establishing the new legislature meant totally ignoring the advice of the Church. In the past Governor Winthrop, more a practical politician than a scholarly theologian, had liked having the Church on his side, observing in 1639: "The elders had great power in the people's heart, which was needful to be upheld, lest the people should break their bonds through abuse of liberty." But when the Church openly entered another dispute in the General Court of March 1644, he reacted angrily: "Some of the elders had done no good offices in this matter, through their misapprehensions both of the intentions of the Magistrates, and also of the matters themselves, being affairs of state, which did not belong to their calling." In other words, the church elders had wandered out of their field of competence.

In the long run of history, however, Massachusetts bequeathed more to modern United States than this reduced authority of the Church, or the 1644 division of the General

Court. These were impressive, but by no means finished accomplishments.*

Instead, the supreme legacy left by the Bay Colony was success in finding multiple ways to check arbitrary government—annual elections, the secret ballot, a written code of laws and liberties, and the possibility of impeaching officials who got out of line.

John Winthrop was the first American official ever to face impeachment proceedings, in May 1645. Possibly inspired by events in England where Parliament was successfully checking the arbitrary one-man government of Charles I, the Bay Colony decided that Governor Winthrop had become a local version of autocratic rule. In the sixteen elections held between 1630 and 1645, he had never been far removed from the reins of power—"Father of New England" Cotton Mather would call him in 1700—and his voice had always sounded loud and clear in any given controversy: Anne Hutchinson, codification of the laws, or the negative voice.

In the October 1644 session of the General Court, he plunged himself into more controversy. He took the extreme position that during periods between sessions of the court, the magistrates were directed by the original company charter of 1629 to act as an executive council, making all necessary decisions as to the day-to-day government of the colony, and

* The religious test for holding office in Massachusetts was removed only in 1820, and not until 1833 was an amendment added to the state constitution formally separating Church and State. As for the bicameral legislature, the precedent for the future United States Congress and for most state legislatures had been set, but for the time being the magistrates still retained the greatest amount of power in the colony, completely in line with John Winthrop's dictum: "The best part is always the least, and of that best part the wiser is always the lesser." The magistrates acted as executive council, court of appeals, and upper chamber of the legislature.

meting out punishment for all offenses committed. To the deputies, this smacked of elitism and undermined their recently won second chamber of the legislature. When the General Court met, the House of Deputies sat as one of two equal branches, so that the people had significant power to restrain the elite group of magistrates. But with Winthrop's interpretation of an executive council, the magistrates reverted to an unchecked position of superiority for a good part of every year.

"John Temper-well" was the most insulting nickname a malicious opponent could find for John Winthrop. And now when the deputies accused Winthrop of foisting arbitrary government on them, he tamed his temper and his tongue by penning a long discourse to show "what arbitrary government was, and that our government (in the state it now stood) was not arbitrary, neither in the ground and foundation of it, nor in the exercise and administration of it."

Pointedly, Winthrop described the difference between an arbitrary government based on human willfulness and a non-arbitrary government: "Arbitrary government is where a people have men set over them, without their choice or allowance; who have power to govern them and judge their causes without a rule. . . . Where the people have liberty to admit or reject their governors and to require the rule by which they shall be governed and judged, this is not an arbitrary government."

Thousands of scholarly words later, after reviewing the original charter and the government that had evolved in Massachusetts, including, ironically, the Body of Laws, which he had himself opposed, he apologized for his wordiness: "This discourse is run out to more length than was intended." Then like a modern commentator summarizing and condensing a lengthy document, he reviewed the highlights at the end: "The conclusion is this. The government of Massachusetts consists of Magistrates and freemen. In the one is placed the authority; in the other the liberty of the commonwealth. Either has power to act, both alone, both together; yet by a distinct power, the one of liberty, the other of authority: the freemen act of themselves in electing their Magistrates and officers; the Magistrates act alone in all occurrences out of court; and both act together in the General Court; yet all limited by certain rules, both in the greater and smaller affairs, so as the government is regular in a mixed aristocracy, and no way arbitrary."

However, Winthrop's eloquence did nothing more than convince his enemies that they needed a more specific charge than general arbitrariness if they were to unseat him forever. "The Governor had by his unspotted *Integrity* procured himself a great Reputation among the *People;* and then the Crime of *Popularity* was laid unto his Charge by such, who were willing to deliver him from the Danger of having *all Men speak well of him.*" The bitterly sarcastic words, with italics that shriek at the reader, came from the turn-of-the-century (1700) pen of Cotton Mather, grandson of two Puritan divines, John Cotton, prominent from the time of his 1633 arrival, and Richard Mather, minister ·of Dorchester, 1636–1669. They were both close associates of John Winthrop.

Like the Puritans in the Long Parliament who had charged giant opponents Archbishop William Laud and the King's chief adviser, the Earl of Strafford, with petty crimes, Winthrop's opponents dug up something to use against the now deputy-governor (though for purposes of banishment in their new land-rich country, not for execution as in England). They accused him of a specific act of arbitrariness—his ordering to prison, when he was governor, two men accused of ignoring the Bay Colony government in a minor dispute involving confirmation of the lieutenant of the Hingham militia.

Woodcut of Richard Mather by John Foster, 1670, earliest portrait engraving executed in English America—Courtesy Massachusetts Historical Society, photographed by George M. Cushing.

Perhaps John Winthrop could have won on the merits of the case. But his friends among the magistrates took no chances. They assured his acquittal through some decidedly shady but sophisticated maneuvering, including selection of a group unanimously favorable to Winthrop to arbitrate the dispute. Cotton Mather ignored such details, reporting with great glee: "The result of that Hearing was, that notwithstanding the touchy *Jealousy* of the People about their Liberties lay at the bottom of all this Prosecution, yet Mr. *Winthrop* was publicly acquitted."

The hearing might have receded into oblivion, except that John Winthrop asked "leave for a little speech" immediately afterward. Speaking with great humility he made it easy for listeners to blot out his lapses into status-quo pigheadedness. They could focus instead on his nearly superhuman achievement in organizing and holding together against formidable odds the Commonwealth of Massachusetts. "When you choose Magistrates you take them from among yourselves, men to like passions as you are. Therefore when you see infirmities in us, you should reflect upon your own, and that would make you bear the more with us, and not be severe censurers of the failing of your Magistrates, when you have continual experience of the life infirmities in yourselves and others. . . . When you call one to be a Magistrate, you must run the hazard of his skill and ability."

With an eloquence born of devotion to the ideals of Massachusetts, and confidence in his own calling, John Winthrop outlined the political theory underlying the role of the magistrates in the power structure of the Bay Colony government, concluding: "It is yourselves who have called us to this office, and being called by you, we have our authority by God." Significantly, he did not claim authority directly from God as did Kings James and Charles. First came the choice of the people and then the "authority from God."

Almost two hundred years later, Alexis de Tocqueville of France, a shrewd political observer, wrote in his study of American society and politics, *Democracy in America:* "A system of legislation without a precedent was produced off-hand by the natural originality of men's imaginations. In the bosom of this obscure democracy, which had as yet brought forth neither generals nor philosophers nor authors, a man might stand up in the face of a free people and pronounce with general applause . . . [a] fine definition of liberty." Then like so many before and since, De Tocqueville quoted from the "little speech," without mentioning the immediate circumstances.

At the time, Massachusetts showered approval on Winthrop's "little speech," which runs to two-and-a-half pages of very small type in his journal. After defeating him for governor in 1644 and 1645, they returned him as chief executive by an overwhelming vote in the next annual election, May 1646.

Undoubtedly this would have been a suicidal time to throw out the colony's most experienced and dedicated leader. Massachusetts was just taking important steps toward true economic independence. The Civil War in England, which had threatened to destroy the New England Puritans at the beginning of the decade by cutting the area off from access to English goods, made them turn inward to developing their own trade and industry. As the decade progressed, they built more of their own ships to export not only fish, furs, and cattle, but such wood products as barrel staves and hoops to Spain for use in her wine industry. And they built ships for sale to other countries. Less and less they looked to agriculture for extra income—always a painful joke anyway because of the barren, rocky soil and harsh winters. Cheerfully an anonymous rhymester had complained (in a ditty passed from lip to lip for over a century till someone finally wrote it down):

Forefathers' Song

New England's annoyances you that would know them

Pray ponder these verses which briefly doth show them.

The place where we live is a wilderness wood,
Where grass is much wanting that's fruitful and good,
Our mountains and hills and our valleys below,
Being commonly covered with ice and with snow.
And when the north-west wind with violence blows,
Then every man pulls his cap over his nose:
But if any's so hardy and will it withstand,
He forfeits a finger, a foot, or a hand.

But when the Spring opens we then take the hoe,
And make the ground ready to plant and to sow.
Our corn being planted and seed being sown,
The worms destroy much before it is grown;
And when it is growing, some spoil there is made
By birds and by squirrels that pluck up the blade;
And when it is come to full corn in the ear,
It is often destroyed by raccoon and by deer.

And now our garments begin to grow thin,
And wool is much wanted to card and to spin;
If we can get a garment to cover without
Our other in-garments are clout upon clout:

Our clothes we brought with us are apt to be torn,
They need to be clouted soon after they're worn,
But clouting our garments they hinder us nothing,
Clouts double are warmer than single whole clothing.

If fresh meat be wanting to fill up our dish,
We have carrots and turnips as much as we wish:
And if there's a mind for a delicate dish
We repair to the clam-banks, and there we catch
    fish.
Instead of pottage and puddings and custards and
    pies,
Our pumpkins and parsnips are common supplies;
We have pumpkins at morning and pumpkins at
    noon,
If it was not for pumpkins we should be undone!

Governor Winthrop's strong sense of direction—now that
duties and rights for leaders and led were well defined—was
also needed to build protection against the world outside.
Sporadically, Massachusetts, and in fact all of New England,
faced threats of attack from the French to the north, the
Dutch on Long Island, and the Swedes around the Delaware
River. And always there were the Indians who showed signs
of restiveness as the white intruders tamed more of the surrounding land.

"A Firm and Perpetual
League of Friendship"

"If we in America should forbear to unite for offense and defense against a common enemy till we have leave from England our throats might all be cut before the messenger would be half seas through."

This thrillerlike description of New England's isolation during the English Civil War was considered no exaggeration in the 1640s. Again history outclassed fiction. Fearing sudden conquest, death, or both, four tiny New England colonies, in a logical and natural sequence—the kind any novelist might strain to contrive artificially—foreshadowed the eventual union of England's Atlantic colonies 130 years later.

The New England colonists had to fend for and defend themselves, a situation they came to accept as difficult but necessary for preserving their independence. All through England's Civil War they were equally leery of King and Parliament, even though their sympathies were clearly with Parliament. The King was too busy warding off the collapse of England at home to offer help, or even give much thought to his overseas "possessions." And they decided to ask for no help from Parliament, because, as John Winthrop explained: "If we should put ourselves under the protection of the Parliament, we must then be subject to all such laws as they should make, or at least such as they might impose upon us; in which course though they should intend our good, yet it might prove very prejudicial to us."

In the process of slurring Parliament and snubbing the King, Massachusetts showed increased interest in the proposal of New Haven and Connecticut for a union of New England settlements. Like England, Massachusetts had become a mother country, spawning several independent daughters. New England, originally planned as one self-governed area, now included colonies at Connecticut, New Haven, and Rhode Island. And in addition there was Plymouth, the pathfinder to New England, always so cordial and helpful to Massachusetts Bay in the stressful early years.

Plymouth had first proposed that Massachusetts join her in colonizing Connecticut in 1633 to ward off Dutch encroachment and because of "three or four thousand warlike Indians" in the area. But little came of the effort. Finally in 1635 a group of Puritan nobles led by Lord Saye and Lord Brooke—the same two men who had thought of emigrating to Massachusetts if the colony met their preconditions—prevailed on John Winthrop, Jr., to settle at the mouth of the Connecticut River where he would become governor of Saybrook. The nobles had no immediate intention of settling there themselves, but wanted the area as a refuge in the event that they had to flee from England.

The following year, forty-nine-year-old Thomas Hooker, pastor of Newtowne, led thirty-five families to settle in the Connecticut valley, around the site of present-day Hartford. This group had mixed motives. They wanted more and better land where they could farm profitably and engage in lucrative fur trade. Besides, a bitter religious dispute over how much independence to allow each individual church had broken out between Boston's conservative minister John Cotton and Newtowne's more liberal Thomas Hooker. Joined with young Winthrop's Saybrook, the new colony obtained a commission from the Massachusetts General Court to govern itself under the Indian-derived name "Connecticut" (with an extra "c" in the middle, which no one has ever pronounced or explained). In 1639 they issued their own written form of government, the Fundamental Orders of Connecticut, generally patterned after the government of Massachusetts. As founder and minister in Hartford, Hooker exercised strong influence on the Connecticut colony in its formative years. And when Hooker died in 1647, Edward Johnson remembered him in poetry:

> Thou angel bright, by Christ for light now made,
> Throughout the world as seasoning salt to be.
> Although in dust thy body smoldering fade,
> Thy head's in heaven, and hath a crown for thee.

Nearby New Haven was settled by a group of Puritan traders from London, under the leadership of the Reverend John Davenport and his wealthiest parishioner Theophilus Eaton. They purchased land from the local Indians, and proceeded to set up a trading post, dangerously close to Long Island Sound, which was under the control of the Dutch. The most staunchly church-oriented of all the New England colonies, New Haven adopted a Frame of Government in 1641, restricting the franchise to church members only, relying exclusively on the Mosaic law for its legal system, and omitting trial by jury (because they could find no reference to trial by jury in the Old Testament).

Rhode Island, first settled by Roger Williams in 1636, and later welcoming the Hutchinsonians, was considered completely heretical by Massachusetts and thus beyond the pale of civilization. Besides, Rhode Islanders were continually quarreling among themselves, so that it took three full years after Roger Williams had succeeded in obtaining a favorable charter from Parliament before they finally came to agreement about putting it into operation. Eventually Rhode Island applied three different times—1644, 1648, and 1655—to join her sister colonies in union, but was turned down.

Likewise, Maine, the domain of royalist Ferdinando Gorges who had caused a great deal of trouble in the 1630s by urging the King and Laud to rescind the Massachusetts Charter of 1629, was considered no friend. Gorges and his province "were not received nor called into the confederation," Winthrop wrote, "because they ran a different course from us both in their ministry and civil administration."

By 1643, the four like-minded and politically similar colonies of Massachusetts, Plymouth, Connecticut, and New Haven agreed to band together as the United Colonies of New England. Massachusetts was the strongest and most populous, with fifteen thousand inhabitants; Plymouth and Connecticut each had three thousand, and New Haven, twenty-five hundred. Delegates meeting at Boston, drew up a confederation agreement, consisting of twelve articles, which was ratified by all four colonies.

Not usually so thrifty with his praise, Edward Johnson used only one poem to glorify both the New England Confederation and one of its founders Theophilus Eaton, also co-founder of the New Haven Colony:

Thou noble thus, Theophilus, before great kings to
   stand,

More noble far, for Christ his war thou leav'st thy
   native land.

. . . .

Our state affairs thy will repairs, assistant thou has
   been
Firm league to make, for Gospel's sake, four colonies
   within;
With Swedes, French, Dutch, and Indians much,
   God's peoples peace this bred. . . .

According to this early document of federalism in America,
the Articles of Confederation of 1643, each of the four New
England colonies would send two representatives to an annual
meeting to determine Indian policy, relations with foreign
countries, and settlement of disputes among themselves. Like
the modern United Nations, they were an international league
of nation states, each one retaining sovereignty, but uniting to
cope with the threat of invasion.

In a blunt preamble, the colonies wrote their reasons for
desiring unity. They had "further dispersed upon the sea coast
and rivers than was at first intended," and thus could not
"with convenience communicate in one government and jurisdiction." They also noted the difficulties of living "encom-
passed with people of several nations and strange languages,"
and of having their fears aroused because the "natives . . . have
of late combined against us" (in the Pequot War). They concluded that "the sad distractions in England" hindered them
"both from that humble way of seeking advice, and reaping
those comfortable fruits of protection which, at other times,
we might well expect. We therefore do conceive it our
bounden duty, without delay, to enter into a present conso-

ciation amongst ourselves for mutual help and strength in all our future concernments. . . ."

Many of the ideas expressed in the Articles of Confederation of 1643 made their way in identical or similar words into the Articles of Confederation of all thirteen colonies in 1781, and from there into the Constitution of the United States. The very first article directed that "it is fully agreed and concluded by and between the parties or jurisdictions . . . that they all be and henceforth be called by the name of the *United Colonies of New England*." The name was derived from "The United Provinces of the Netherlands," familiar to many New Englanders from their residence there. Until the Declaration of Independence, all thirteen colonies referred to themselves as the United Colonies. And the first article of the 1781 Confederation of the Thirteen Colonies read: "The style of this confederacy shall be *The United States of America*."

Article II in 1643 proclaimed: "The said United Colonies for themselves and their posterities do jointly and severally hereby enter into a firm and perpetual league of friendship and amity, for offense and defense, mutual advice and succour, upon all just occasions . . . for their own mutual safety and welfare." Substituting "states" for "colonies," Article III, 1781, is strongly imitative: "The said states hereby severally enter into a firm league of friendship with each other, for their common defense, the security of their liberties, and their mutual and general welfare, binding themselves to assist each other, against all force offered to, or attacks made upon them . . . ."

By 1787, the preamble to the United States Constitution read: "We the people of the United States, in order to form a more perfect union, establish justice, ensure domestic tranquillity, provide for the common defense, promote the general welfare, and secure the blessings of liberty to ourselves and our posterity, do ordain and establish this constitution for the United States of America." There is certainly a strong family resemblance between the Articles of Confederation of 1643, the Articles of Confederation of 1781, and the United States Constitution of 1787.

In 1643, all four colonies were assured of retaining "jurisdiction and government within their limits." In 1781, each of the thirteen states retained "sovereignty, freedom and independence, and every power, jurisdiction and right which is not by this confederation expressly delegated to the United States, in Congress assembled." By 1787 the infant United States had learned by trial and error of the Confederation that the central government must be strengthened, yet by 1791 thought it necessary to add as the Tenth Amendment: "The powers not delegated to the United States by the constitution, nor prohibited by it to the states, are reserved to the states respectively, or to the people."

The Confederation of 1643 probably saved the Constitutional Convention of 1787 from dying a quick death on the issue of taxation. Benjamin Franklin, at eighty-one still going strong as a chief compromiser at that convention, is known to have scribbled an analysis of the Confederation of 1643 on his proposed draft of an earlier constitution in 1775. Dr. Franklin, an inveterate reader who had spent the first seventeen years of his life in Boston as a printer, and Rufus King and John Adams, both of Massachusetts, all often "expressed an indebtedness to the early Confederation." As a representative for Massachusetts at the Constitutional Convention in 1787, Rufus King proposed—and Dr. Franklin pushed—the convention-rescuing compromise, part of which included taxing each state proportionally according to population as determined by census. These ideas of proportional taxation and census originated in the Articles of Confederation of 1643.

The present-day United States Senate owes a great deal to the New England Confederation of 1643. Today each state regardless of size or population has two voting senators. This can be traced directly to the practice of two representatives and equal votes for each of the four colonies at the annual meeting of the Confederation. Also, the Senate, established in 1787 to represent the states, whereas the House of Representatives would represent the people directly, was given powers that the states had exercised under the Articles of Confederation of 1781, which in turn derived from similar prerogatives claimed by the four colonies in 1643. For example, today the Senate has the power to give "advice and consent" on foreign policy providing "two thirds of the Senators present concur." All the way back in 1643 the four colonies exercised the same power, with "any six of the eight agreeing." And in 1781 the requirement was that "nine [out of thirteen] states assent to same."

Other contributions of the United Colonies of New England, 1643, to the modern United States of America included the federal idea of the coexistence of state and national governments, each with their specific spheres of action; war powers, including the declaration of war, and the raising of necessary taxes and armies; annual meetings; prohibition of forming new states out of already existing ones, except by consent of the state involved; supervision of relations with the Indians; return of criminals to the site of the crime, and return of fugitive servants (an unhappy precedent for the writing of the fugitive slave law into the body of the United States Constitution—Article IV, Section 2); and careful enumeration of powers to be exercised.

The idea of a supreme court also originated with the Confederation. John Winthrop wrote: Connecticut's Governor Edward Hopkins "said it was nothing to them what the General Court had done in the Bay: for the Court of Commissioners [two from each colony] was the supreme court and what they did must stand."

The Confederation of 1643, like the Confederation of 1781, disdained an elected executive or president. Convinced that the King was the source of their troubles in both eras, they looked to the exercise of legislative powers by the main body of government (Commissioners in 1643, Congress in 1781), with executive and judicial duties incidental to the scheme of government. The idea worked better in the seventeenth century than in the eighteenth. For almost half a century the first Confederation succeeded reasonably well, and thus encouraged the newly independent United States to attempt to repeat the experiment in federal unity with the Articles of Confederation of 1781.

But four struggling colonies with a population of 24,000, nominally part of the seventeenth-century British Empire, were far removed in time, circumstance, and history, from thirteen states of a newly born eighteenth-century nation of 2,500,000. The Confederation of 1643 gave rise to an elaborate and expanded imitation in 1781. However, the Confederation of 1781 could only point to the need for a strong constitution, separated into legislative, executive, and judicial branches, each checking and balancing the other to prevent tyranny. Yet the Founding Fathers, meeting in Philadelphia in 1787, used their experience under the Confederation as their guide. They kept unchanged what worked well in the Articles of Confederation, made additions and improvements where indicated by necessity, and threw out the unworkable. Without the Confederation experiences of 1643 and 1781, they could not have known how to proceed in framing the world's oldest written constitution still in use. And without the Massachusetts Body of Laws, the Bay Colony Charter and government, and the English Revolution, the four New England colonies could never have developed the first Articles of Confederation.

The new Confederation began functioning just in the nick of time in the spring of 1643.

"You English Massachussians"

Civil war back "home" affected New England very directly. On at least two separate occasions some iconoclastic New Englanders might have tumbled the entire structure of government, except that 3,000 miles away in England King and Parliament were bent only on exterminating each other. First there was Samuel Gorton, who struck even his fellow Rhode Islander Roger Williams as a radical in religion. Caught between conflicting land claims of Roger Williams and Massachusetts Bay, both of whom coveted the area Gorton and his ten followers had cleared for settlement and religious experiment, Gorton stubbornly defied the commissioners of the United Colonies (his case was brought before them as a quarrel between Massachusetts and the "foreign state" of Rhode Island), and was thrown into prison. Later he attempted to cause more trouble by traveling to England to appeal directly to Parliament to support his cause by ordering charter recall.

Failing in his appeal to an otherwise preoccupied Parliament, Gorton won points with posterity through his poetry:

> Then walk through sea or land, by friends or foes
> Let Prisons fast, hard irons thee, inclose,
> All take thy part, yea, plead thy cause for thee;
> The world vents its malice, in Christ's love thou are
> free.

Shortly afterward there was the Remonstrance and Humble Petition, presented to the Massachusetts General Court by Robert Child, considered as much a troublemaker as Roger Williams or Anne Hutchinson. Looking to the increasing success of Parliament in liberalizing English politics, he demanded greater participation of nonfreemen in government, found the relationship between Church and State still too close, and denounced Massachusetts's independence of England. Child was a thirty-three-year-old doctor, a graduate of Cambridge University in England, who had taken a degree in medicine at the University of Padua, Italy. He had first visited New England in the early 1640s, and returned to England where he viewed for himself the accomplishments of Parliament. He came back to Massachusetts in 1645, demanding closer ties with England and with Parliament; increased religious toleration for those who disagreed with the civil authorities; and a further liberalizing of the right to vote by removing the qualification that only members of the Established Puritan church could become freemen, entitled to vote for members of the General Court or themselves hold office.

Anticipating rejection by the General Court, he and his cohorts threatened to take the one step which from the very beginning had haunted the Bay Colony government with visions of complete downfall. Dr. Child and his friends warned that if Massachusetts laws were not brought into accord with the laws of England they would "be necessitated to apply their humble desires to the honorable Houses of Parliament, who, they hoped, would take their sad condition into their serious considerations."

Glumly, Edward Johnson described the purpose of the petition: "To stir up the people to dislike of the present government . . . inveighing against the constitution of the government as not popular enough . . . [or] against the laws or orders of this little commonwealth as too strict. . . ."

Whatever else, Dr. Child succeeded in stirring up the General Court. They sent Edward Winslow, a magistrate of neighboring Plymouth, to present their side of the story to Parliament. This was 1646, and flushed with success in uniting the New England colonies and with their own independence, Massachusetts instructed Winslow to tell Parliament in no uncertain terms: "Our charter gives us absolute power of government."

Winslow arrived in England before word of Dr. Child's demands could reach Parliament. He convinced Parliament that Massachusetts knew exactly what it was doing and should be allowed to continue unhampered (not a difficult request for Parliament to grant at a time when it was busy defending itself militarily against the King's forces).

The Child Petition required radical reaction, Massachusetts decided, and so even before Winslow could return with an answer, the colony fined and imprisoned Child and his associates. Child fought back, resting his position on the right of free petition. "They were not questioned for petitioning," the General Court responded, "but for such miscarriages, etc., as appeared in their petition and remonstrance."

Claiming arbitrary arrest, Child demanded to know the charge. The court refused, asserting that the charge would be revealed in due time, but that the imminent departure of Child

Edward Winslow—Courtesy of the Pilgrim Hall Museum, Plymouth, Massachusetts.

and his associates had made immediate arrest imperative. In his journal John Winthrop contended: "They complained of fear of perpetual slavery, but their intent was to make us slaves to them." Governor Winthrop and his fellow magistrates were still captives of the medieval concept of unity. They lacked the confidence—bred of deep and permanent roots—that would allow them to experiment with liberty of dissent.

The Magistracy, however, reserved different treatment for the less articulate Thomas Fowle, a co-conspirator with Child, and a church member who had no interest in becoming a freeman—"too much trouble and charge." After bailing himself out of prison, he was allowed to embark for England, taking with him copies of the paper that Child had submitted to the General Court and the petition to Parliament (after Winslow had been given sufficient time to put Massachusetts's case to Parliament first).

Before Fowle left, John Cotton, as leading Boston minister, claimed advance knowledge about the course of the voyage. In a dramatic sermon he terrorized all those about to embark along with Fowle. On the high seas, to the horror of all those who had been brave enough to depart anyway, Cotton's prediction began coming true. A man-killing storm erupted, seemingly to punish those who carried complaints against God's chosen people in Massachusetts Bay. In panic, fellow passengers prevailed on Fowle to throw the offending papers overboard. He had several copies of the petition originally submitted to the General Court, so to quiet the superstitious, he gave them one to throw on the water. Several hours passed before the "sacrifice" took effect, but after safe arrival in England, some of the passengers spread the word that there had been a miracle at sea.

The Child petition, as delivered by Thomas Fowle, was largely ignored in England. But the very challenge of the petition caused the Massachusetts General Court to think through the colony's position in relation to England—in words which sound strikingly similar to those used in the Declaration of Rights of the First Continental Congress in October 1774, just twenty-one months before the Declaration of Independence.

In 1646, the Massachusetts General Court replied to the Child petition: "They charge us with breach of our charter and of our oaths of allegiance, whereas our allegiance binds us not to the laws of England any longer than while we live in England, for the laws of the Parliament of England reach no further, nor do the King's writs under the great seal go any further." In 1774 the Continental Congress declared: "The foundation of English liberty, and of all free government, is a right in the people to participate in their legislative council. And as the English colonists are not represented, and from their local and other circumstances cannot properly be represented in the British Parliament, they are entitled to a free and exclusive power of legislation in their several provincial legislatures." John Adams, a member of the committee that drew up this document for the Congress—his great-great-grandfather had emigrated from Devonshire, England, to Massachusetts Bay around 1636—wrote a year later in 1775: "However it may sound, I say we are not part of the British empire, because the British government is not an empire. . . . America will never allow that Parliament has any authority to alter their constitution at all. She is wholly penetrated with a sense of necessity of resisting it at all hazards. . . . The question we insist on most is, not whether the alteration is for the better or not, but whether Parliament has any right to make any alteration at all. And it is the sense of America that it has none."

In 1646, Dr. Child lost his case. He was forced to pay a fine, to serve a prison sentence, and finally to return to England. Abruptly, in 1647, the General Court did an about-face.

Magistrates and deputies passed legislation allowing nonfreemen to vote for town officers, and to run for the office of town selectman—as long as the majority of selectmen elected were freemen. Nonfreemen would still be forbidden to vote for deputies or magistrates of the General Court. However, since most men rarely left their communities, and seldom had business dealings outside their immediate residence, town government and the ability to participate in it were far more important to the individual inhabitant than the remote General Court. Continuing this reform fervor, a few years later Massachusetts removed town and commonwealth government from Boston's church-meetinghouse to a specially erected townhouse. The well-defined separation of Church and State that Child had demanded was not yet complete, but the Bay Colony had taken definite steps in that direction.

Protected from invasion by the Confederation of the New England Colonies, and from encroachments on their charter by the civil war in England, Massachusetts Bay reached a new plateau of stability and self-confidence in the late 1640s. Anne Bradstreet, whose husband Simon was now serving his seventeenth year as Massachusetts assistant, found the security and contentment, nestled among her family of four sons and four daughters, to write an entire book of verse. In a long dedication, filled with sentiment but concluding simply, she honored her father, Thomas Dudley, always in service to Massachusetts as governor, deputy governor, or assistant:

> From her that to your self more duty owes
> Than water in the boundless ocean flows.

Her brother-in-law, Reverend John Woodbridge of Andover, took her poetry to London in 1647, where it was published three years later, whimsically titled, *The Tenth Muse*

Lately Sprung up in America, and subtitled, *Or Several Poems, compiled with a great variety of Wit and Learning, full of delight ... By a Gentlewoman in those parts.*

Gently, Anne Bradstreet aimed some of her "Wit" at the likes of Nathaniel Ward and John Winthrop who, in spite of increasing emphasis in the post-Renaissance world on individual dignity, considered servants, women, and girl children, less than human:

> I am obnoxious to each carping tongue
> Who says my hand a needle better fits,
> A poet's pen all scorn I should thus wrong,
> For such despite they cast on female wits;
> If what I do prove well, it won't advance,
> They'll say it's stol'n, or else it was by chance.

By 1647, emerging from the tumult over Samuel Gorton, Robert Child, and the hearings on John Winthrop's arbitrariness, the Bay colonists showed every sign of knowing exactly where they wanted to go and how they wanted to get there. Two months after the final departure of Dr. Child to England, they passed legislation requiring a teacher for every town of fifty families or more, and a grammar school for every town of at least one hundred families. Funds would come from the public treasury by way of direct taxes on private property (according to early Massachusetts records). The following year, 1648, they codified ecclesiastical discipline in the Cambridge Platform of Church Discipline, and produced The Laws and Liberties of Massachusetts, "one of the crowning achievements of the Bay Colony," according to George Lee Haskins of the University of Pennsylvania, author of the landmark study, *Law and Authority in Early Massachusetts*.

The new code revised and expanded the Body of Liberties

of 1641, adding laws still in force but omitted from the earlier code, as well as laws newly enacted. Three lawyers were in charge of drawing up the new code—John Winthrop, who had so vociferously opposed the Body of Liberties, but apparently had since come to appreciate its magnificent achievement (perhaps since his own brush with the authorities on arbitrariness); Nathaniel Ward, who had drawn up the earlier code and was preparing to retire to England; and Richard Bellingham, the learned lawyer who had opposed and defeated John Winthrop for governor on this very issue of written laws in the election of 1641.

Their method was to pair well-defined civil responsibilities with civil liberties, and to make full use of all constitutional developments arising from the commonwealth's eighteen years of experience in self-government. They emphasized the idea of higher law and joined together the law of nature and the law of God, exactly as Thomas Jefferson did 128 years later when he justified declaring independence from England on the basis of the "laws of nature and of Nature's God."

Throughout the document, this learned and politically sophisticated trio reaffirmed their basic belief that the law consists of logic as well as experience. And they included prohibitions against such sins as lying, drinking to excess, gambling, idleness, and unfair trade. Dangerously, the State took over policing morality, since religion no longer dictated every aspect of life.

With an innocence that contrasts sharply with the twentieth-century picture of the arrogant, self-righteous Puritan, they described the new code:

For if it be no disparagement to the wisdom of that High Court of Parliament in England that in four hundred years they could not so compile their laws and regulate proceedings in the courts of justice, etc., but that they had still new work to do of the same kind almost every Parliament, there can be no just cause to blame a poor colony (being unfurnished of laws and statesmen) that in eighteen years hath produced no more, nor better rules for a good and settled Government than this book holds forth; nor have you (our brethren and neighbors) any cause, whether you look back upon our native country, or take your observations by other states, and commonwealths in Europe, to complain of such as you have employed in this service; for the time which hath been spent in making laws, and repealing and altering them so often, nor of the charge which the country hath been put to for those occasions, the civilian gives you a satisfactory reason of such continual alterations, additions, etc.

The code contained considerable borrowing of English laws and English court practices. It was "an authoritative compilation of constitutional provisions and civil administration—justice, courts, trade, taxation, licensing, agriculture, education, military affairs, and the relations between church and state." Also it contained "much substantive law relating to such matters as crime, inheritance, and domestic relations."

With the code as his final monument and his entire life in New England dedicated to the service of Massachusetts Bay, John Winthrop died at the age of sixty-one on March 26, 1649. He had won election nineteen times to the Magistracy —twelve years as governor, three as deputy governor, and four as assistant. And twice he was named presiding officer of the United Colonies of New England, during its very first year of existence, 1643, and again in 1645.

A little more than a century after the death of John Winthrop, in 1764, historian Thomas Hutchinson, royal Governor of Massachusetts and great-great-grandson of the banished Anne Hutchinson, circulated a long-lived legend: "Some writers say, that upon his [Winthrop's] death-bed, when Mr. Dudley pressed him to sign an order of banishment of an heterodox person, he refused, saying 'he had done too much of that work already.' "

Perciful Lowle, seventy-eight-year-old merchant from Bristol, England, and ancestor of the Massachusetts Lowells, wrote his only known verse, eulogizing John Winthrop at the time of the Governor's death. The eulogy, ninety-eight lines long, begins:

> You English Massachussians all
> Forbear sometime from sleeping,
> Let everyone both great and small
> Prepare themselves for weeping.
> For he is gone that was our friend,
> This Tyrant Death hath wrought his end
> Who was the very chief among
> The chiefest of our peers
> Who hath in peace maintained us long
> The space of nineteen years.

Lowle ends his verse humbly, and for poetic rhythm uses the modern spelling of his name:

> Here you have Lowells loyalty
> Penned with his slender skill
> And with it no good poetry
> Yet certainly good will.
> Read these few verses willingly
> And view them not with *Momus* eye

Friendly correct what is amiss
Accept his love that did write this.

There is no record that anyone ever informed John Win-throp of the recent, violent death of King Charles I of Eng-land, January 30, 1649.

"Un-Kingship is Proclaimed"

Long hair is for "ruffians and barbarous Indians," decreed the Massachusetts General Court in the spring of 1649. "We hereby . . . do declare and manifest our dislike and detestation against the wearing of such long hair, as against a thing un-civil and unmanly, whereby men do deform themselves, and offend sober and modest men, and do corrupt good manners."

Obviously, Massachusetts Puritans were allowing themselves the luxury of playing with legislation on less than a life-or-death level. Nineteen years of attention to every minute detail of strong self-government had produced spectacular results—already imitated by Plymouth, Connecticut, and New Haven, and highly touted in the mother country, too.

The Bay Colony's confidence and self-respect kept bursting into print for all to read and see. Reverend Peter Bulkeley, a founder of Concord, Massachusetts, who had been minister at Woodhill, England, rhapsodized: "We have that plenty and abundance of ordinances and means of grace, as few people enjoy the like."

218

And back in England, in 1651, the son of Dorchester's minister Richard Mather, Nathaniel, wrote of the special esteem showered on New Englanders: " 'Tis a notion of mighty great and high respect to have been a New-English man, 'tis enough to gain a man very much respect, yea, almost any preferment. . . . Myself within less than three hours of my coming to the city had two offers."

But when all was said and done, the years 1649–1660 in New England—and maybe even more so in old England—turned out to be a period of frightening uncertainty and weak politics.

In Massachusetts, John Endecott succeeded, but hardly replaced, the late John Winthrop as Governor in the annual election of May 1649. Best remembered as the impetuous old soldier who had cut the red cross out of the king's flag, Endecott was elected governor thirteen more times and deputy governor twice over the next fifteen years, till his own death in 1664 at the age of 74. Reliable, loyal, but sometimes dangerously inflexible, he turned out to be nothing more nor less than caretaker of Massachusetts, in a period which varied from consolidation to confusion.

Meanwhile in England, royalist John Evelyn, sounding for all the world like Alice in Wonderland that same May of 1649, announced to his diary: "Un-kingship was proclaimed, and his Majesty's statues thrown down at St. Paul's Portico and the Exchange." He referred to the two months' series of acts by the Rump Parliament, starting on March 17, 1649, "abolishing the office of King" as "unnecessary, burdensome, and dangerous to the liberty, safety, and public interest of the people, and that for the most part, use hath been made of the regal power and prerogative to oppress and impoverish and enslave the subject."

Two days later Parliament had abolished the House of

Lords as "useless and dangerous to the people of England." And on May 19, 1649, they summed up all these previous acts with "An Act Declaring England to be a Commonwealth" . . . proclaiming that henceforth they would be governed as "a Commonwealth and Free state, by the supreme authority of this nation, the representatives of the people in Parliament, and by such as they shall appoint and constitute as officers and ministers under them for the good of the people, and that without any King or House of Lords."

Yet with all this grand talk of a free state, the Rump Parliament did not dare to call an election—which almost certainly would have gone against them. And almost their first administrative act was to silence the extreme democrats, known as the "Levellers." This was the group demanding universal suffrage, religious toleration, and freedom of speech.

Fifty-year-old Oliver Cromwell was now in charge of the Rump—and of all England. He had been a member of Parliament at the age of thirty, and a soldier only when he reached his early forties. But he finally reached the heights of political leadership through his military victories over the King. And for the rest of his life he proved more successful as soldier than as politician.

Almost at once, New Englanders began treating their fellow Puritan on the other side of the Atlantic politely, but with extreme wariness. They resented Cromwell's persistent attempts to involve them in his various wars for preservation of the English commonwealth, or in his schemes for imperialist expansion. Their first falling-out with Cromwell came shortly after the death of King Charles, when the Irish problem, never settled in the 1640s, exploded into new rebellions against the occupation troops of the Protestant English. In a whirlwind campaign, 1649–1650, Cromwell reconquered Ireland—massacring thousands of Catholics at Drogheda and Wexford—and

Oliver Cromwell, captioned His Highness Effigies standing in state
—Courtesy National Portrait Gallery, London.

proceeded to pursue a policy highly reminiscent of the hated Strafford fifteen years before. Mourning the fate of his countrymen, an Irish poet cried:

> The Gael are being wasted, deeply wounded,
> Subjugated, slain, extirpated,
> By plague, by famine, by war, by persecution,
> It was God's justice not to free them,
> They went not together hand in hand.

Having massacred and subdued the Irish, Cromwell insulted Bay colonists with his request that a sizable number remove themselves to Ireland for permanent settlement there. With no understanding of their pride of accomplishment and strong feelings of patriotism for their New England home, he suggested that in Ireland they could still have the adventure of being colonists, and would, in addition, reap the supreme benefit of being much closer to their native England. He made quite clear his admiration for Massachusetts's strong display of organization and perseverance, exactly the qualities needed to insure Ireland against invasion from any hostile European powers intent on proving to their own subjects that royal execution had no future.

Politely the Massachusetts General Court in October 1651 thanked Cromwell for his "tender care and undeserved respect," but gently reproved him for having "occasioned some discouragement and weakening to the whole body of the colony [which] necessarily brings an ill report upon the land, as if defective in that which makes for a people's comfortable subsistence." If any individuals wanted to go on their own, they concluded, that would be easy to arrange. "Our intent is only to let your excellence understand [our] state and condition."

Cromwell's next crisis was the invasion from hostile Scotland led by Prince Charles, son of the beheaded King. The Prince was decisively beaten at Worcester in September 1651, and fled to the Continent, reaching port by slinking from the shelter of one Catholic house to another. This time Boston agreed to a Cromwell request, accepting 270 Scottish prisoners. They were cared for by their fellow countrymen already living in the Bay capital, or taken as indentured servants, allowed to become freemen after working off their servitude.

Ironically, Cromwell's next foreign policy move, the Navigation Act of 1651, limiting English shipping to English or English colonial carriers, was aimed at old Puritan friends and Calvinist brethren, the Dutch. This act, first in a series of similar acts, was aimed at strengthening England at the expense of the Netherlands. It had no real effect on New Englanders, except perhaps to inflate their notions of privileged character status—something they felt coming to them because of their Puritanism. The southern, non-Puritan colonies of Virginia, Maryland, Barbados, and Bermuda, docilely obeyed the letter of the law. But with old England too busy to take time for enforcement, New England got away with setting her own rules and regulations for trading with all nations.

Naval rivalry between England and the Netherlands, along with England's attempt to enforce the Navigation Act, erupted into war. And New England faced another crisis. The Netherlands was across the Channel from England; but for New England it bordered on the colonies of Connecticut and New Haven (most exposed and most nervous about its Dutch neighbors). The United Colonies, with the conspicuous exception of Massachusetts, were more than willing to fight the Dutch navy in local waters, and to attack New Netherland under Cromwell's orders and supervision.

Massachusetts, supremely idealistic or selfishly villainous depending on the point of view, refused to obey Cromwell's orders or to go along with the majority decision of the United Colonies. Feeling so confident and independent that in 1652 she declared herself a commonwealth with exactly the same rights and privileges of sovereignty as the Commonwealth of Great Britain, her motive for nullification of a United Colonies decision was either (1) hatred of war, (2) reluctance to fight fellow Protestants, especially the ones who had given her people aid and shelter when needed so desperately, or (3) lack of a common border and therefore no conflict over land. In any case, Massachusetts had caused the first nullification crisis in American history, different in time but not in kind from similar crises which brought on the American Revolution in the 1770s or the Civil War between North and South in 1861.

Very much like the modern United Nations, the now ten-year-old Confederation had worked perfectly until confronted with an emergency, at which point its lack of a central power to enforce the will of the majority almost strangled it. Only the conclusion of peace between the Dutch and Cromwell, on terms favorable to England, saved the Confederation. And Massachusetts could turn near-catastrophe around into a precocious pursuit of an independent foreign policy—based on benefit to herself, with no thought to the effect on England.

After triumphing over the Dutch, Cromwell turned his attention to governing Great Britain, leaving New England alone until 1655. Then he again insulted New Englanders by requesting their resettlement in another part of the British Empire, Jamaica in the Caribbean, recently conquered from Spain. Unsuccessfully, he tried to entice Puritan colonists with liberal grants of land and descriptions of an ideal climate.

Massachusetts, highly experienced in the art of stalling since the crises in the 1630s over returning her charter to King Charles, took almost a year to respond. Then, honeying their letter with a "thankful acknowledgment of His Highness's Favor," the General Court firmly refused Cromwell's offer.

Cromwell dropped the matter, busying himself instead with reclaiming England from anarchy and with further empire-building. He decided that he had finally had enough of the Rump. And on April 20, 1653, he dismissed what remained of the Long Parliament, which had first met on November 3, 1640. In the company of several musketeers from his own regiment, he appeared in the chamber as Parliament was trying to put through a bill to perpetuate itself forever and give its members unlimited power. Shouting insults, he pointed to one member, "There sits a taker of bribes." To another, he screamed, "There sits a man whose religion is a farce." And to another he roared, "There sits a man whose personal conduct is impure and foul." He finished: "You are no Parliament. I say you are no Parliament. I will put an end to your sitting." With twenty or so soldiers following him, he stomped up and down the chamber driving members out. Only the widespread popular hatred for the Rump Parliament, and gratitude for Cromwell's military prowess, saved Cromwell from accusations of treason or capriciousness.

Exactly eight months later Cromwell set himself up as Lord Protector of the Commonwealth of England, Ireland, and Scotland. This was the first time all of the British Isles had been joined in one political union (though the union lasted only during Cromwell's lifetime).

Cromwell, as Lord Protector, struggled long and hard for a constitutional basis of government. However, he made no headway. Parliament refused to ratify his constitution, called the "Instrument of Government," and the nation indi-

Bulstrod and Whitlock present to Oliver the Instrument of Government—from 52 "playing cards" cartoons of the Cromwell interregnum—Courtesy of the Trustees of the British Museum, London.

cated that it still craved a king as ruler, several times offering the kingship to Cromwell. Preferring the title Lord Protector, Cromwell steadfastly refused the Crown, but found other royal prerogatives impossible to turn down: a more sumptuous style of dress, the right to name his own successor, and a form of address as "His Highness."

As Lord Protector, Cromwell managed to govern England until his death early in the autumn of 1658. Domestically, his great accomplishment was supplying the necessary breathing space after pulling down the ancient structure of government. In fact, the only real political and constitutional successes of the Puritan Revolution were achieved by John Pym, leader of Parliament from its summoning in 1640 to his death in 1643, a period when Cromwell was still an ordinary Parliamentary backbencher.

During his short rule as Protector, Oliver Cromwell unleashed, from the very top level of government, the seeds of future toleration of such radically dissenting groups as Catholics, Jews, and Quakers. His championing of religious toleration was too premature to be put into practice immediately, though in what amounted to acceptance of political toleration, he succeeded in calming down the murderous passions against dissenters from the established order, which had been aroused by the Civil War. And in 1655 he readmitted Jews to England, the first time they had been allowed to take up residence since their expulsion in 1290.

Cromwell's chief legacy to England turned out to be military might. After beating back all the early threats from abroad to his rule in England, he sent the English navy to police the Mediterranean and so dominate the coasts of Catholic Italy, France, and Spain. The Mediterranean fleet, and a British navy able to rule the world's seas, marked the rise of the worldwide British empire, which held sway until the early twentieth century. Cromwell's contemporary, Edmund Waller, a former royalist poet, offered paeans to Cromwell's naval policy:

> The sea's our own; and now all nations greet,
> With bending sails, each vessel of our fleet;
> Your power extends as far as winds can blow,
> Or swelling sails upon the globe may go.

As his successor, Oliver Cromwell left behind his son Richard. But "Tumbledown Dick" had absolutely no qualifications to rule, and allowed the army to seize control. Confusion followed anarchy, until a weary and discouraged army began to look longingly at Charles II, living in exile. George Monk, serving as General of the Protectorate's forces in Scotland, and

A Free state or a tolleration for all sort of Villany.

A free state or a toleration for all sorts of villany, from 52 "playing cards" cartoons of the Cromwell interregnum—Courtesy of the Trustees of the British Museum, London.

strongly loyal to Oliver Cromwell and his memory, awaited a signal from Richard Cromwell that he planned to rule. Instead, Monk later explained in self-justification: "Richard Cromwell forsook himself, else I had never failed my promise to his father or my regard to his memory."

Ingeniously, Monk engineered a *coup d'état* without bloodshed. Returning from his military post in Scotland, he called the old Rump Parliament into session, and summoned back also the members excluded in Pride's Purge. Thus reconstituted, Parliament became much more conservative and pro-monarchy. They legislated the formalities of restoring the monarchy and delegated a mission to Holland to invite Charles to return as King Charles II of Great Britain, after promising in his Declaration at Breda, April 4, 1660, that he would grant "liberty of tender consciences" and allow Parliament to punish offenders.

Disillusionment with the Cromwell interregnum had engulfed even staunch Puritans. Lucy Hutchinson, writing the memoirs of her husband John, Puritan colonel during the Civil War and one of fifty-nine who had sat in judgment of Charles I and signed his death warrant, complained:

Cromwell and his army grew wanton with their power and invented a thousand tricks of government, which, when nobody opposed, they themselves fell to dislike and vary every day. . . . He at last exercised such an arbitrary power, that the whole land grew weary of him, while he set up a company of silly, mean fellows, called major-generals, as governors in every county. These ruled according to their wills, by no law but what seemed good in their own eyes, imprisoning men, obstructing the course of justice between man and man, perverting right through partiality, acquitting some that were guilty, and punishing some that were innocent as guilty. . . . At last he took upon himself to make lords and knights, and wanted not many fools, both of the army and gentry, to accept of, and strut in, his mock titles.

Less vindictive, royalist John Evelyn, while offering no love for Oliver Cromwell, found that his foreign policy had passed the test of success: "His greatness at home was but a shadow of the glory he had abroad. It was hard to discover, which feared him most, France, Spain, or the Low Countries, where his friendship was current at the value he put upon it." Grudgingly concluding that posterity would look on Cromwell as a "brave bad man," Evelyn reported that the Protector, against the advice of his council, had decided not to immerse the country in the blood of King Charles's supporters. Snidely, Evelyn added to his diary, "maybe out of too much contempt for his enemies."

Hugh Peter, who in 1652 was enthusiastically writing to his old New England friends to return to England, by 1654 was advising them to stay put because of England's "great uncertainty and changes." By 1658, in the anticlimax of the Cromwell interregnum, he was writing, "Truly upon all accounts, I think New England best, if clothing and bread may be had."

"Our Sovereign Lord the King"

Massachusetts took no official notice of Oliver Cromwell's death. The offers of kingship to the Lord Protector, coming on top of his various attempts to involve New Englanders in empire-building, made them refuse to mourn him publicly.

For a private reaction to Cromwell's death, however, there is the diary of Boston goldsmith John Hull: "We received the sad news of the death of the Lord Protector, Oliver Cromwell, a man of excellent worth, who died September 3, 1658. The Lord give suitable affections to bewail the loss of such choice ones! He was one that sought the good of New England; though he seemed to be wanting in a thorough testimony against the blasphemers of our days."

John Hull's reaction to Cromwell's death may or may not have expressed typical private sentiment. In any case, John Hull had special reason to note Cromwell's passing. The Protector's failure ever to protest Massachusetts's unprecedented decision to coin its own money, a prerogative exercised only by sovereign nations, had given Hull special standing in

The Pine Tree Shilling, dated 1652. The spelling of "Massachu-setts" in the enabling legislation and on the actual coin are re-markably different.

the community, and a place in history too. By order of the General Court on June 10, 1652, Massachusetts had estab-lished its own mint, with this very same John Hull as mint-master.

Twenty-eight when he received this historically unique appointment, Hull was almost a second-generation settler, hav-ing first arrived in the colony at the age of ten with his immi-grating father in 1634. As mintmaster, his instructions were to acquire "bullion, plate, or Spanish coin," which he was to convert "into twelve-penny, six-penny, and three-penny pieces, which should be for form flat and square on the sides, and stamped on the one side with N. E. and on the other side with xii^d, vi^d, and iii^d, according to the value of each piece, together with a privy mark, which should be appointed every three months by the Governor, and known only to him and the sworn officers of the mint." Three months after passage of the act, this money, containing three-quarters of the silver contained in English coinage of the same denominations, was declared legal tender. Later in the same year it was voted that "for the prevention of washing or clipping . . . that henceforth all pieces of money coined as aforesaid should have a double ring on either side, with this inscription, *Massachusetts*, and a tree in the center, on one side; and *New England*, and the year of our Lord, on the other side." For more than thirty years this coinage was continued, always using "1652," the date of the year in which the mint was established. Massachusetts had solved for herself the problem of a shortage of coin necessary for commerce and at the same time strengthened her position as the center of New England trade.

The year that Massachusetts began coining her own money was the same year that she officially proclaimed herself an independent commonwealth. Her spirits and intentions were high, but unfortunately with the turn of events in England and the deaths of many of New England's founders, this decade witnessed the last gasps of independence.

Massachusetts lost John Cotton, December 23, 1652. "If Boston be the chief seat of New England," wrote minister-historian-diarist Cotton Mather, his grandson, "it was Cotton that was the father and glory of Boston." His chief contribution was intense loyalty to the late Governor Winthrop—whom Cotton, obviously liking the father image, had called "father of New England." Revealing something of his character, as well as the hardships of homesickness, amidst his uprooting from Boston, England, and resettlement in Boston, Massachusetts, Cotton left behind an eight-line verse:

> When I think of the sweet and gracious company
> That at Boston once I had,
> And of the long peace of a fruitful Ministry
> For twenty years enjoy'd:
>
> The joy that I found in all that happiness
> Doth still so much refresh me,
> That the grief to be cast out into a wilderness
> Doth not so much distress me.

The following year, Thomas Dudley, seventy-seven years

old, who had twice defeated John Winthrop for the governorship and had served thirteen times as deputy governor, and
five as assistant, died on July 31, 1653. Cotton Mather included
in his diary a long poem supposedly found in Dudley's pocket,
entitled, "A New England Gentleman's Epitaph":

> Dim eyes, deaf ears, cold stomach show
> My dissolution is in view;
> Eleven times seven near lived have I,
> And now God calls, I willing die:
> My shuttle's shot, my race is run,
> My sun is set, my deed is done;
> My span is measur'd, tale is told,
> My flower is faded and grown old,
> My dream is vanish'd, shadow's fled,
> My soul with Christ, my body dead;
> Farewell dear wife, children and friends,
> Hate heresy, make blessed ends;
> Bear poverty, live with good men,
> So shall we meet with joy again.
>
> Let men of God in courts and churches watch
> O'er such as do a toleration hatch;
> Lest that ill egg bring forth a cockatrice,
> To poison all with heresy and vice.
> If men be left, and otherwise combine,
> My epitaph's, *I died no libertine.*

Another kind of rhyme found its way to the tombstone of
Theophilus Eaton of New Haven, governor for 19 years
since the very beginning of that colony, who died January 7,
1658:

> Eaton, so famed, so wise, so meek, so just,

The Phoenix of our world, here hides his dust;
This name forget England never must.

Plymouth and its Governor William Bradford were not spared either. After thirty-seven years of courageous and indispensable service to Plymouth and all of New England, Governor Bradford died on May 9, 1657. At the age of sixty-eight he left behind the New World's first literary masterpiece, the journal of the settlement of Plymouth, *Of Plymouth Plantation.* In 1702 Cotton Mather wrote in his *Magnalia Christi Americana*, a history of New England: "Governor Bradford was "lamented by all the colonies of New England as a common blessing and father to them all."

The deaths of so many founders in New England, together with the transition and uncertainty in New England, made the 1650s go out not with a whimper but with shrieking disgrace. Massachusetts hanged four Quakers, whose reputation for causing riots among opposing street crowds in England had preceded their arrival in the New World. Again the Bay commonwealth had reverted to the medieval concept of unity of Church and State as a comforting substitute for strong roots in history or for a securely established government. (Parliament, even under Puritan control and thus supposedly sympathetic to their New England brethren, threatened at least once to revoke the Massachusetts charter.) "Satan made another assault upon God's poor people here, by stirring up the Quakers to come amongst us, both Men and Women," explained Roger Clap, writing his *Memoirs* of the early, difficult decades in Massachusetts for his six children.

With memories still fresh of the banishment of Roger Williams, Anne Hutchinson, and Dr. Robert Child, the Commonwealth of Massachusetts told the Quakers to conform or get out. There was no room for dissent. The gentle Quakers who refused military service, and held a disrespectful attitude for the sacred ceremonies and services of all other Christian sects, appeared as monsters to the Puritans, frightening them with apparent contempt for civil magistrates.

In July 1656, mintmaster John Hull reflected the common attitude toward the Quaker sect in his diary: "This summer two women called Quakers came from Barbados, intending to oppose the ministry and also to breed in people contempt for magistracy, but were cut short of their intents, being kept in prison until opportunity were of sending them whence they came. They were persons uncivil in behavior, showing no respect to any, ready to censure and condemn all; themselves would be thought the only knowing persons and their spirit infallible, carrying a semblance of humility, but extremely proud."

When legislation failed to keep the Quakers out in the first place, or to send them packing once they managed to enter, the Massachusetts General Court by a single vote in a hotly contested session passed a law that anyone convicted by a special jury to be a Quaker should "be sentenced to banishment upon pain of death." Captain Clap applauded this law in his *Memoirs* as "made for our Peace and Safety."

But the sentence of banishment, which had always worked so well in the past, failed this time, and the Bay Colony hanged two ardent young men, William Robinson and Marmaduke Stevenson. Under circumstances amounting to the worst of medieval torture, the court forced Mary Dyer to watch her companions' hanging, blindfolded her, and put a noose around her neck, only to reprieve her at the last moment on the intercession of her son. But Mary Dyer, an old friend and follower of Anne Hutchinson, refused to recant and was finally hanged on Boston Common, June 1, 1660. Her hanging was followed nine months later by the hanging of William Leddra who attempted to appeal to English law, only to be told by a cock-sure Massachusetts General Court that England had no jurisdiction in this case.

In the midst of this Quaker persecution in Massachusetts, Charles II landed at Dover, England, May 25, 1660, to reclaim the throne of England for the Stuart dynasty. "Our private meeting kept a day of humiliation at our house for the state of our native country," observed John Hull when the news reached Massachusetts, "it being like to come . . . under the bishops; the Church countenancing the old liturgy and formalities again to be practiced."

The return of Charles II to the throne of England pushed the Puritans off center-stage both in England and America. But they had been there long enough to change the direction of the world with their legacy of representative government based on the consent of the governed, and their emphasis on the dignity of each individual.

In England, Puritans were persecuted right out of existence. Edward Hyde, Earl of Clarendon—the same man who wrote the highly quotable *History of the Rebellion and the Civil Wars*—had his name attached, not altogether justifiably, to the Clarendon Code. This was a series of four Parliamentary statutes, passed between 1661 and 1665, excluding Puritan Nonconformists from any role in local or central government. These laws were far more stringent and worse for the Puritans than any that Archbishop William Laud had put into effect. But in the 1660s, in contrast to the 1630s when Laud's power was at its peak and Parliament was not even in session, Parliament had now seesawed to the higher position in government. So there was hope for the future.

Puritan reaction was to deemphasize the religious struggle, and concentrate instead on continuing the political struggle for permanent Parliamentary supremacy in old England and for retaining independence in New England. Charles I had ascended the throne in 1625, claiming kingship by divine right, but had suffered smashing defeat on the battlefield. And then he had had his head cut off, just as any ordinary mortal criminal. If religion could not save a divine king, then politics must be the answer for the problem of living together in society. An unknown satirist even represented the new king as thinking along these same lines:

> I'll have a religion all of my own
> Whether Popish or Protestant shall not be known,
> And if it prove troublesome I will have none.

By overwhelming consensus the King had been restored to the throne. But by an equally overwhelming consensus he would never be able to rule again without Parliament. Charles II returned to England as the creature of Parliament—a Parliament that had been summoned by no king, but instead had been put together by the machinations of George Monk. Punster John Collop summed up the whole situation, incidentally indicating the revised standings of politics and religion:

> Our English Monk hath here converted more
> Than all your monks perverted heretofore.

The years between 1640, when the Long Parliament was summoned into session, and 1660, when the kingship was restored, had been filled in equal parts with actual experiments, fertile ideas, and major disappointments. Parliament had learned well the art of government and had forever ended the threat of an absolute monarchy being established in England. In addition, the two decades produced proposals for reform so far ahead of their times that they finally went into effect one

Charles II, studio of Wright, ca. 1660–65—Courtesy of the National Portrait Gallery, London.

hundred, two hundred, and even three hundred years later: toleration, a national bank, law reform, disestablishment of the Church, free trade, free press, women's suffrage, and equal electoral districts.

To men and women still alive and politically conscious in 1660, however, discouragement must have overshadowed accomplishment. The final act of the Cromwellian tragedy in England was played out on January 31, 1661. Oliver Cromwell, never a king in lifetime, but buried with all regal honors, royally costumed "and crowned with a crown, sceptre, and globe, like a king" amidst England's heroes in Westminster Abbey—on page 334 of John Evelyn's diary—was exhumed sixteen pages and fifteen months later—on page 350: "This day (O the stupendous and inscrutable judgments of God!) were the carcasses of those arch-rebels, Cromwell, Bradshawe (the judge who condemned his Majesty), and Ireton (son-in-law to the Usurper) dragged out of their superb tombs in Westminster among the Kings, to Tyburn, and hanged on the gallows there from nine in the morning till six at night, and then buried under that fatal and ignominious monument in a deep pit; thousands of people who had seen them in all their pride being spectators." It took more than 200 years for strong feelings to subside sufficiently to allow erection of a statue outside Parliament of Oliver Cromwell carrying Bible and sword. Facing directly opposite, across the street above a side door to Westminster Abbey is a small bust of the martyred Charles I—a gently ironic finale to a murderous rivalry.

Amid disillusionment and controversy over Cromwell—robust enough to span the centuries—Charles II had no particular need for vengeance or vindictiveness. Or perhaps the newly restored King was simply following the precedent set by Cromwell himself in avoiding a bloodbath, once his regime had replaced the monarchy. Whatever the reason, as Charles had promised in his Declaration at Breda, he gave amnesty to all antiroyalists, unless specially condemned by Parliament. In the end, Parliament excepted only twenty-six from this general amnesty, including three who escaped to Massachusetts and lived out their natural lives, moving from one place to another in New England, sheltered by various individuals against royal expeditions sent to ferret out their hiding places.

For New England, these regicides—heroes when they had sat in judgment of the King and signed his death warrant, but now hunted men—were poignant human symbols of the Restoration in England. Additional and equally poignant reminders came with reports of the extreme torture and painful execution inflicted on two former Bay colonists who had not signed the death warrant. Henry Vane, once governor of Massachusetts, was put to death by torture, not for execution of the King, but for his role in handing over the notes to Parliament that caused the execution of Charles I's minister, the Earl of Strafford. Similarly half-hanged, then disemboweled and quartered while still alive, Hugh Peter, stepfather-in-law of John Winthrop, Jr., and former minister of Salem, was condemned for his enthusiastic sermons urging death for the King. Even though he took no part in the official proceedings, his activities had attracted enough attention to inspire wide circulation of a bitter couplet, twisting the pronunciation of his name to make it rhyme with Jupiter:

> The best man next to Jupiter
> Was put to death by Hugh Peter.

For a whole year after England had restored its monarchy, Massachusetts held off official recognition of Charles II—in a kind of reflex action aimed at preserving its independence. Still acting out the role of sovereign state, the General Court first sent to England for presentation to Charles a document headed "Concerning Our Liberties." They explained that their charter was "the first and main foundation of our civil polity here." They described their governor and company as "a body politic, in fact and name, . . . vested with power to make freemen . . . [who] have the power to choose annually a governor, deputy governor, assistants, and their select representatives or deputies." They pointed out that this "government is privileged, by all fitting means, (yea if need be) by force of arms, to defend themselves," and concluded that only laws repugnant to the laws of England could be discarded. Tampering with other laws enacted by Massachusetts would "be an infringement of our right."

The second half of what they called "The Court's Declaration of their Rights by Charter," June 10, 1661, tactfully spelled out their "duties of allegiance to our sovereign lord the King" —including allegiance to the (still not officially proclaimed in Massachusetts) King, and the promise that "any, legally obnoxious, and flying from the civil justice of the state of England shall come over to these parts, they may not here expect shelter." This sounded impressive, but amounted to the promise by one sovereign state to return criminals at the request of another friendly sovereign state.

Two months later, when the General Court was certain that Charles had had enough time to receive and digest their special situation, Massachusetts officially recognized Charles as King, but carefully avoided mentioning the names of their own or any of the other colonies in their proclamation.

Aftermath

Sophisticated, opinionated, and self-sufficient, Massachusetts had by the time of the Restoration in 1660, learned to live by her wits politically, and by the sea economically. She had become New England's leader in resistance to the English government, as well as the center of trade for all colonies in the area. Unlike any other colony, her settlers had arrived fully equipped with their own charter of independent self-government in 1630, and had been left virtually undisturbed for a full generation. Outside New England, other colonies arrived beholden to England financially for subsidizing their establishment, and were expected to return profit on what amounted to a commercial trading corporation.

Just about a year after his arrival back in England as King, Charles II began giving signs that he intended to rule as well as reign over his New England colonies. Seizing on Massachusetts's weakest display of independence—her law, passed by a single vote in the General Court, to rid the Commonwealth of Quakers by banishment or death—Charles demanded, in September 1661, an end to further executions of these dissenters and the return to England of anyone found "obnoxious." In this instance, Massachusetts decided that Quakers were hardly worth testing the Commonwealth's right to make and enforce their own laws. Hastily they released the offending dissenters from prison, with instructions to go to other colonies, but not to England.

The King next aimed his fire and attention at New Haven, the colony that had aroused his anger by showing extreme hospitality to the escaped regicides. Possibly with the conniv-ance of Connecticut, he demanded unification into one colony of New Haven and Connecticut. This, of course, was com-pletely contrary to the provision of the Articles of Confedera-tion of 1643, which had forbidden the forceful absorption of one member colony by another.

Charles's action proved to be the mortal blow from which the Confederation never could recover, although it remained more or less in existence until 1684. The final attempt at united action by the New England colonies, reduced from quartet to trio, came with the outbreak of King Philip's War in 1675, a war that they fought with no outside help. (Philip, son of Massasoit, who had been so helpful to the Pilgrims in the early days of Plymouth, was sachem of the Wompanoag tribe.) The war erupted out of abrasive culture conflict, which in-cluded different attitudes toward law and order, crime and punishment, and land use. After wholesale slaughter on all sides, including both white and Indian civilian populations, the white man "won," and New England pushed Indians into their first reservations.

By 1684, the Confederation had fended off Indian attack, and acted as a central government for the New England colo-nies in setting the value of money, devising a uniform standard of weights and measures, raising money to finance Harvard

College, and building intercolonial roads. But this was the last year of its existence.

The King had had quite enough of independence and insolence. From inside the royal court, diarist John Evelyn, referring to all of New England as one colony in 1671 when he was made a Commissioner of Plantations, described the area as "very independent as to their regard to Old England or his Majesty," and displaying a "peevish and touchy humor." Repeatedly the King sent commissioners across the Atlantic to reign in New England, and repeatedly the commissioners proved no match for the colonies, highly experienced for over a generation in evading and avoiding requests for returning or revising their charters. Finally the·King saw himself forced to take the step threatened but thwarted from the very beginning of New England's existence. He revoked the precious Massachusetts Bay Charter in 1684.

However, before he could deal with the rest of New England he died. His brother James II, three years younger and a self-proclaimed Catholic succeeded him. Almost immediately James went about ignoring Parliament at home and tightening his hold on New England across the Atlantic. In September 1685, he appointed a temporary governor for Massachusetts, and in December 1686, he sent over as royal governor, Sir Edmund Andros, former governor of New York. Eleven months later, Andros forced all New England colonies, plus New York and New Jersey (both part of the former Dutch colony of New Netherland conquered by Charles II from the Netherlands in 1664), and Pennsylvania to unite into one large royal colony. Henceforth they would be known and treated as the Dominion of New England, under his governorship.

During the four hectic years of 1685–1689, New England found no escape from the maelstrom of old England's affairs. The first year of James's reign, 1685, showed him misreading the national temper and disregarding recently reinforced and anciently preserved British constitutional tradition. Even so, the English people might have suffered through his kingship, because waiting in the wings was his only child, Mary, rigorously raised as a Protestant, and married to her cousin, William of Orange, Prince of the Netherlands and a member of the Stuart family. Princess Mary was James's daughter by his first wife, Anne Hyde, daughter of Edward Hyde, Earl of Clarendon, historian and royal adviser. But Anne Hyde had died in 1671, and been succeeded in 1672 by a new wife, the staunchly Catholic Mary of Modena who, in June 1688, after a series of stillbirths, gave birth to a healthy son. The threat of a Roman Catholic dynasty galvanized leading Whigs and Tories into forgetting their differences and forming a secret alliance which aimed at coronation of Princess Mary of Orange as Queen of England.

When the Princess made known her intention never to accept any position that would place her above her husband, both Houses of Parliament declared the throne vacant, and on February 6, 1689, proclaimed William and Mary joint King and Queen of Great Britain. The influence of the Puritan Revolution made itself heavily felt in this transaction, reinforcing the precedent that the people had chosen their own rulers and consequently had the right to depose and replace those who misgoverned. (This was a concept used by Thomas Jefferson eighty-seven years later in the Declaration of Independence.)

Overseas, Massachusetts carefully followed every development of what nineteenth-century English historian Thomas Babington Macaulay exuberantly dubbed the "Glorious Revolution" of 1688. As early as December 1688, rumors of the planned invasion of William of Orange reached Boston. By March 1689, Bostonians had received word of William's success, although they had to wait until May for full details. However, even the sketchy outline of William's actions was enough to incite rebellion, and on April 18 in Boston (largest city in the most populous and most prosperous colony, and hence the seat of government), the citizenry rose up and overthrew Governor Andros. This was the end of the Dominion of New England, but right up to the Declaration of Independence of 1776, Massachusetts would have a series of royally imposed governors, with the right to review all legislation and exercise veto power over the Council, which was elected by the General Court. As a consolation prize, the new charter, granted by King William to Massachusetts in 1691, gave her control over Plymouth and Maine, Acadia (Nova Scotia), and the islands of Nantucket and Martha's Vineyard (formerly part of New York).

In her years of complete independence, 1630–1660, Massachusetts had had an immediate influence on the surrounding New England colonies that had branched out from the original Bay Colony. And when Delaware, Pennsylvania, New Jersey, and New York, came into existence in the second half of the seventeenth century, "the prevailing temper of the Middle Colonies," early twentieth-century English historian George Trevelyan noted, 'resembled the Puritan democracy of the North." A later twentieth-century legal historian, George L. Haskins of the University of Pennsylvania, pointed out that when England won New York from the Dutch, the Province of New York studied Massachusetts law for precedents as well as the code of Connecticut, which was based on Massachusetts law.

A strong legislature and a penchant for reducing laws to writing—beginning with the Massachusetts Body of Laws and Liberties of 1641—and a first attempt at colonial unity through the United Colonies of 1643, were helpful precedents when the colonies declared independence from England in 1776 and established American constitutional government. The English had liberated themselves from an arbitrary king, placing him under control of the more representative government of Parliament. The future United States had to cast aside an English king, and in addition had to replace the rule of Parliament, in which America could not physically be represented, by her own national legislature, Congress.

However, in the meantime, all was not lost for Massachusetts even during the years following King William's imposition of a new charter in 1691. Massachusetts had learned well the art of politics. The royally appointed governor had to depend on the General Court for his salary. And therein lies a whole new tale of how once-independent Massachusetts loped along, a quasi-independent colony until at least 1760.

A Note on Sources, Citations, and Seventeenth-Century Spelling and Dates

Listed below are, first, the contemporary or near-contemporary diaries, histories, letters, official documents, poetry, and edited collections, which have been used extensively in *Kings, Commoners, and Colonists*. Second are the nineteenth- and twentieth-century books that have proved most informative and helpful. Last, a few periodical articles are included.

Quotations in the text of the book fall into several categories. Those from the seventeenth or eighteenth centuries are so full of color and of the author's personality that their identification becomes an integral part of the narration. In the same way, a few instances of unique twentieth-century interpretation or research have required on-the-spot identification. On the other hand, a comprehensive bibliography of sources used seems the best guide to many quotations, particularly in the cases of poetry or anecdotes, which have become part of the folklore of their own times.

Where identification of a highly significant interpretation or quotation is essential, but might have interrupted the flow of narration, acknowledgment has been made in the section following the bibliography.

Seventeenth-century spelling has been modernized, with the sense left intact. Also, as pointed out in the Prologue, England's Julian calendar was ten days behind Europe's Gregorian calendar. No attempt has been made to modernize dates, except to follow common twentieth-century usage in beginning the year on January 1, rather than in late March as the English of the seventeenth century did. Thus, in Chapter Ten the date of the King's execution is given as January 30, 1649. To give the date as January 30, 1648, would be accurate but confusing. January and February were considered the last two months of the year in seventeenth-century England, which of course explains the Latin origins of the still-used names, September, October, November, and December—seventh, eighth, ninth, and tenth months.

Sources

CONTEMPORARY AND NEAR-CONTEMPORARY SOURCES

(Please note that these have been alphabetized according to the main subject. Thus, *Chronicles of the First Planters of the Colony of Massachusetts Bay* is listed under "M" for Massachusetts Bay. Except for Anne Bradstreet, other contemporary poets cited have been anthologized, and so are included in a separate section at the end of this section, alphabetized according to editor.)

The Annals of America, Vol. I, 1493–1754. Encyclopedia Brittanica, Inc.: Chicago, 1968.

American History Told by Contemporaries, Vol. I, Albert Bushnell Hart, ed. The Macmillan Company: New York, 1964.

Great Issues in American History, 1584–1776, Clarence L. Ver Steeg and Richard Hofstadter, eds. Vintage: New York, 1969.

A Source Book in American History to 1787, Willis Mason West, ed. Allyn and Bacon: Boston, 1913.

Works of Anne Bradstreet, John Harvard Ellis, ed. Peter Smith: Gloucester, Mass., 1962.

Bradford, William, *Of Plymouth Plantation*, Samuel Eliot Morison, ed. Random House, Modern Library: New York, 1952.

The Chamberlain Letters, Elizabeth Thomson, ed. G. P. Putnam's Sons: New York, 1965.

Characters from the Histories and Memoirs of the Seventeenth Century, David Nichol Smith, ed. Oxford: London, 1963.

The Letters of King Charles I, Sir Charles Petrie, ed. Funk and Wagnalls: New York, 1968.

Memoirs of Roger Clap. Reprinted by Books for Libraries Press: Freeport, N.Y., 1971.

Clarendon, Selections from the History of the Rebellion and Civil Wars, G. Huehns, ed. Oxford: London, 1968.

The Commonwealth of England, 1641–1660, Charles Blitzer, ed. G. P. Putnam's Sons: New York, 1963.

The Constitutional Documents of the Puritan Revolution, 1625–1660, Samuel R. Gardiner, ed. Oxford: London, 1968.

Constitutional Documents of the Reign of James I, 1603–1685, J. R. Tanner, ed. Cambridge University Press: Cambridge, England, 1961.

Evelyn, John, *Diary,* William Bray, ed. 2 Vols. Dutton, Everyman's Library: New York, 1966.

Hakluyt, Richard, *The Principal Navigations, Voyages, Traffiques and Discoveries of the English Nation Made by Sea or Over-land to the Remote and Farthest Distant Quarters of the Earth at any time within the compasse of these 1600 Yeeres,* Irwin R. Blackmer, ed. The Viking Press: New York, 1965.

Hubbard, William, *A General History of New England from the Discovery to 1680.* Collections of the Massachusetts Historical Society, second ser., Vols. V–VI.

The Diaries of John Hull, Vol. III Archeologica Americana, American Antiquarian Society: Worcester, Mass.

Hume, David, *The History of Great Britain, The Reigns of James I and Charles I.* First published 1754. Penguin: Middlesex, England, republished 1970.

Hutchinson, Lucy, *Memoirs of the Life of Colonel Hutchinson,* the Rev. Julius Hutchinson, ed. Dutton, Everyman's Library: New York, 1965.

Hutchinson, Thomas, *History of the Colony and Province of Massachusetts Bay,* Lawrence Shaw Mayo, ed. 3 vols. Harvard University Press: Cambridge, Mass., 1936.

Johnson's *Wonder-Working Providence,* 1628–1651, J. Franklin Jameson, ed. Barnes and Noble: New York, 1910.

Chronicles of the First Planters of the Colony of Massachusetts Bay, Alexander Young, ed. Da Capo Press: New York, 1970.

Cotton Mather Selections, Kenneth B. Murdock, ed. Hafner Publishing Company: New York, 1965.

Chronicles of the Pilgrim Fathers, Alexander Young, ed., Charles C. Little and James Brown: Boston, 1841.

Milton's Prose, Malcolm W. Wallace, ed. Oxford: London, 1925.

Puritan Political Ideas, Edmund S. Morgan, ed. Bobbs-Merrill: Indianapolis, 1965.

The Puritans, A Sourcebook of Their Writings, Perry Miller and Thomas H. Johnson, eds. 2 vols. Harper Torchbooks: New York, 1963.

Smith, John, *The Generall Historie of Virginia, New-England, and the Summer Isles*. University Microfilms, Inc.: Ann Arbor, Mich., 1966.
(Note: Since this reproduction of the original version has more flavor than legibility, a reasonable substitute, in modern type and spelling, is *The Colonial Image*, John C. Miller, ed. George Braziller: New York, 1962. Specifically see pages 66–75: "Captain John Smith, A Description of New England.")
The Stuart Constitution, J. P. Kenyon, ed. Cambridge University Press: Cambridge, England, 1969.
The Genesis of the United States, Alexander Brown, ed. 2 vols. Russell and Russell: New York, 1964.
The Life and Times of Anthony à Wood, Andrew Clark and Llewelyn Powys, eds. Oxford: London, 1961.
Life and Letters of John Winthrop, Robert C. Winthrop, ed. 2 vols. Little, Brown and Company: Boston, 1869.
Winthrop Papers, Allyn B. Forbes, ed. 5 vols. Russell and Russell: New York, 1968.
Winthrop's Journal History of New England, 1630–1649, James Kendall Hosmer, ed. 2 vols. Barnes and Noble: New York, 1959.
Wood, William, *New England's Prospect*. London, 1634. Reprinted, 1865.

ANTHOLOGIES OF CONTEMPORARY POETS

Hale, Edward Everett, *New England History in Ballads*. Little, Brown and Company: Boston, 1904.
Jantz, Harold S., *The First Century of New England Verse*, Russell and Russell: New York, 1962.
Untermeyer, Louis, *Early American Poets*. Library Publishers: New York, 1952.
Wedgwood, C. V., *Poetry and Politics under the Stuarts*. University of Michigan Press: Ann Arbor, Mich., 1964.

NINETEENTH- AND TWENTIETH-CENTURY BOOKS

Adams, Brooks, *The Emancipation of Massachusetts*. Houghton Mifflin: Boston, 1962.

Adams, Charles Francis, *Three Episodes of Massachusetts History*. Russell and Russell: New York, 1965.

Adams, James Truslow, *The Founding of New England*. The Atlantic Monthly Press: Boston, 1921.

Aiken, Conrad, *Collected Poems*. 2d ed. Oxford: New York, 1970.

Akrigg, G. P. V., *Jacobean Pageant*. Harvard University Press: Cambridge, Mass., 1963.

Andrews, Charles M., *The Colonial Background of the American Revolution*. Yale University Press: New Haven, 1964.

Andrews, Charles M., *The Colonial Period of American History*. 4 vols. Yale University Press: New Haven, 1964.

Ashley, Maurice, *England in the Seventeenth Century*. Penguin, Baltimore: 1961.

Aylmer, G. E., *A Short History of Seventeenth Century England, 1603–1689*. Mentor: New York, 1963.

Bailyn, Bernard, *The New England Merchants in the Seventeenth Century*. Harper Torchbooks: New York, 1964.

Barbour, Philip L., *The Three Worlds of Captain John Smith*. Houghton Mifflin: Boston, 1964.

Battis, Emery, *Saints and Sectaries*. University of North Carolina Press: Chapel Hill, 1962.

Billias, George A., ed., *Law and Authority in Colonial America*. Barre Publishers: Barre, Mass., 1965.

Bindoff, S. T., *Tudor England*. Penguin: Baltimore, 1967.

Black, Robert C., III, *The Younger John Winthrop*. Columbia University Press: New York, 1966.

Bridenbaugh, Carl, *Vexed and Troubled Englishmen, 1590–1642* Oxford: New York, 1968.

Brinton, Crane, *The Anatomy of Revolution*. Vintage Books: New York, 1960.

Burton, Elizabeth, *The Pageant of Elizabethan England*. Charles Scribner's Sons: New York, 1962.

Burton, Elizabeth, *The Pageant of Stuart England*. Charles Scribner's Sons: New York, 1962.

Cheyney, Edward Potts, *European Background of American History, 1300–1600*. Collier: New York, 1966.

Colbourn, H. Trevor, *The Lamp of Experience*. University of North Carolina Press: Chapel Hill, 1965.

Davies, Godfrey, *The Early Stuarts*, 1603–1660. Oxford: London, 1959.

De Tocqueville, Alexis, *Democracy in America*. 2 vols. Vintage Books: New York, 1945.

Dow, George F., *Every Day Life in Massachusetts Bay Colony*. The Society for the Preservation of New England Antiquities: Boston, 1935.

Dunn, Richard S., *Puritans and Yankees*. W. W. Norton: New York, 1962.

Earle, Alice Morse, *Colonial Dames and Good Wives*. Houghton Mifflin: Boston, 1895.

Earle, Alice Morse, *Margaret Winthrop*. Charles Scribner's Sons: New York, 1896.

Felt, Joseph B., *Defence of Hugh Peters*. C. C. P. Moody: Boston, 1851.

Firth, Sir Charles, *Oliver Cromwell and the Rule of the Puritans in England*. Oxford: England, 1968.

Fiske, John, *The Beginnings of New England*. Houghton Mifflin: Boston, 1889.

Gooch, G. P., *English Democratic Ideas in the Seventeenth Century*. Harper Torchbooks: New York, 1959.

Gookin, Frederick W., *Daniel Gookin, 1612–1687*. Privately printed. Chicago, 1912.

Haller, William, *Liberty and Reformation in the Puritan Revolution*. Columbia University Press: New York, 1967.

Hart, Albert Bushnell, ed., *Commonwealth History of Massachusetts*. The States History Company: New York, 1927/1928.

Haskins, George Lee, *Law and Authority in Early Massachusetts*. Macmillan: New York, 1960.

Hibbert, Christopher, *Charles I*. Harper and Row: New York, 1968.

Hill, C. P., *England, 1603–1714. Who's Who in History*. Vol. III. Basil Blackwell: Oxford, 1965.

Hill, Christopher, *The Century of Revolution*. W. W. Norton: New York, 1966.

Hill, Christopher, *God's Englishman, Oliver Cromwell and the English Revolution*. Pelican: London, 1972.

Hill, Christopher, *Intellectual Origins of the English Revolution*.

Panther: London, 1966.

Hill, Christopher, *Puritanism and Revolution*. Panther: London, 1968.

Hillary, A. A., *Oliver Cromwell and the Challenge to the Monarchy*. Pergamon Press: Oxford and London, 1969.

Howe, Henry F., *Prologue to New England*. Farrar and Rinehart, Inc.: New York, 1962.

Jernegan, Marcus Wilson, *The American Colonies, 1492–1750*. Frederick Ungar Publishing Co.: New York, 1959.

Kenyon, J. P., *The Stuarts*. Collins: London, 1970.

Langdon, George D., Jr., *Pilgrim Colony*. Yale University Press: New Haven, 1966.

Macaulay, Thomas Babington, *The History of England*. Vols. I–IV, Phillips, Sampson: Boston, 1852–1856; Vol. V, Crosby, Nicols, Lee: Boston, 1861.

Mayo, Lawrence Shaw, *John Endecott*. Harvard University Press: Cambridge, Mass., 1936.

McIlwain, Charles Howard, *The American Revolution, a Constitutional Interpretation*. Cornell University Press: Ithaca, N.Y., 1958.

McLaughlin, Andrew C., *Foundation of American Constitutionalism*. Fawcett: New York, 1961.

Miller, Perry, *Orthodoxy in Massachusetts, 1630–1650*. Harper Torchbooks: New York, 1970.

Miller, Perry, *Roger Williams*. Atheneum: New York, 1970.

Morgan, Edmund S., *The Puritan Dilemma, The Story of John Winthrop*. Little Brown: Boston, 1958.

Morgan, Edmund S., *Visible Saints*. Cornell University Press: Ithaca, N.Y., 1968.

Morison, Samuel Eliot, *Builders of the Bay Colony*. Houghton Mifflin: Boston, 1958.

Morison, Samuel Eliot, *The European Discovery of America*. Oxford: N.Y., 1971.

Morison, Samuel Eliot, *The Intellectual Life of New England*. Cornell University Press: Ithaca, N.Y., 1960.

Newton, Arthur P., *The Colonising Activities of the English Puritans*. Kennikat Press: Port Washington, N.Y., 1966.

Northend, William D., *The Bay Colony*, Estes and Lauriat: Boston, 1896.

Notestein, Wallace, *The English People on the Eve of Colonization, 1603–1630*. Harper Torchbooks: New York, 1962.

Oman, Carola, *Henrietta Maria*. Hodder and Stoughton: London, 1936.

Osgood, Herbert L., *The American Colonies in the Seventeenth Century*. Peter Smith: Gloucester, Mass., 1957.

Palfrey, John Gorham, *History of New England*. 3 vols. Little Brown: Boston, 1865.

Perry, Ralph Barton, *Puritanism and Democracy*. Vanguard Press: New York, 1944.

Pomfret, John E., *Founding of the American Colonies, 1583–1660*. Harper Torchbooks: New York, 1970.

Rutman, Darrett B., *Winthrop's Boston*. University of North Carolina Press: Chapel Hill, 1965.

Saunderson, Henry Hallam, *Puritan Principles and Democratic Ideals*. The Pilgrim Press: Boston and Chicago, 1930.

Savelle, Max, *The Foundations of American Civilization*. Henry Holt: New York, 1942.

Simpson, Alan, *Puritanism in Old and New England*. The University of Chicago Press: Chicago, 1970.

Smith, Bradford, *Captain John Smith*. J. P. Lippincott: Philadelphia, 1953.

Stewart, George R., *Names on the Land*. Houghton Mifflin: Boston, 1967.

Stone, Lawrence, *The Causes of the English Revolution, 1529–1642*. Routledge and Kegan Paul: London, 1972.

Tanner, J. R., *English Constitutional Conflicts of the Seventeenth Century, 1603–1689*. Cambridge University Press: Cambridge, England, 1962.

Thornton, John Wingate, *The Historical Relation of New England to the English Commonwealth*. Privately printed by Alfred Mudge: Boston, 1874.

Trevelyan, George M., *England under the Stuarts*. G. P. Putnam's Sons: New York, 1914.

Vaughan, Alden T., *New England Frontier, Puritans and Indians, 1620–1675*. Little, Brown: Boston, 1965.

Ver Steeg, Clarence, *The Formative Years, 1607–1763*. Hill and Wang: New York, 1964.

Ward, Harry M., *The United Colonies of New England, 1643–1690*. Vantage Press: New York, 1961.

Wedgwood, C. V., *The King's Peace, 1637–1641*. Collier: U.S.A., 1969.

Wedgwood, C. V., *The King's War*. Collins: London, 1958.

Wedgwood, C. V., *The Trial of Charles I*. Fontana: London, 1957.

Wertenbaker, Thomas Jefferson, *The Puritan Oligarchy*. Grosset and Dunlap: New York, 1947.

Willson, David Harris, *King James VI and I*. Oxford University Press: New York, 1967.

Winslow, Ola Elizabeth, *Meetinghouse Hill, 1630–1783*. Macmillan: New York, 1952.

Wright, Louis B., *The Atlantic Frontier*. Cornell University Press: Ithaca, N.Y., 1959.

Wright, Louis B., *The Cultural Life of the American Colonies, 1607–1763*. Harper Torchbooks: New York, 1962.

Zagorin, Perez, *The Court and the Country*. Atheneum: New York, 1970.

ARTICLES APPEARING IN MODERN PERIODICALS

Brown, B. Katherine, "A Note on Freemanship in Puritan Massachusetts." *American Historical Review*, Vol. 59 (1954): 865–883.

Brown, B. Katherine, "Puritan Concept of Aristocracy." *Mississippi Valley Historical Review*, Vol. 41 (1954–55): 105–112.

Gray, Stanley, "The Political Thought of John Winthrop." *New England Quarterly*, III (1930): 235–250.

Haskins, George L., and Ewing, Samuel E., III, "The Spread of Massachusetts Law in the Seventeenth Century." *University of Pennsylvania Law Review*, Vol. 106 (1958): 413–418.

McIlwain, Charles H., "The Transfer of the Charter to New England and Its Significance in American Constitutional History." *Massachusetts Historical Society Proceedings*, Vol. 63 (1929): 53–64.

Mosse, George L., "Puritanism and Reason of State in Old and

New England." William and Mary *Quarterly*, IX (1952): 67–81.
Sache, William L., "Migration of New Englanders to England." American Historical Review, Vol. 53 (1948): 251–278.

Attributions Not Included in the Text

CHAPTER TWO, p. 25: "pleaseful, wise, learned. . . ." David Harris Willson, *King James VI and I.*

CHAPTER THREE, p. 38: John Cabot was "the first discoverer of North America since the Northmen's voyages almost five centuries earlier." Samuel Eliot Morison, *The European Discovery of America.* (The comment on the French claim to Canada in 1608 relies on the same source.)

p. 40: Hakluyt's voyages "have been well called the prose epics of the English nation." *Ibid.*

p. 50: "Current catechism on the Pilgrim's destination." Cf. George D. Langdon, Jr., *Pilgrim Colony;* John E. Pomfret, *Founding the American Colonies;* and William Bradford, *Of Plymouth Plantation.*

CHAPTER SIX, p. 93: Quotes on Arbella and Isaac Johnson, taken from William Hubbard, *A General History of New England.*

pp. 103 and 104: Material on Indians from Alden Vaughn, *New England Frontier.*

p. 106: Care of poor, Darrett B. Rutman, *Winthrop's Boston,* esp. pp. 217, 218, 219–20, 258.

CHAPTER SEVEN, p. 115: Massachusetts' special flag. Richard S. Dunn, *Puritans and Yankees.*

CHAPTER EIGHT, p. 132: Indiscriminate use of "Mrs." Alice Morse Earle, *Colonial Dames and Good Wives.*

CHAPTER TEN, p. 166: Oliver Cromwell legend from Sir Charles Firth, *Oliver Cromwell*.

CHAPTER THIRTEEN, p. 202: Benjamin Franklin's familiarity with the Articles of Confederation of 1643, from Harry M. Ward, *The United Colonies of New England*.

CHAPTER FIFTEEN, p. 220: Quote on the familiarity with New England codes, Sir Charles Firth, *Oliver Cromwell*.

p. 230: Quotes by Hugh Peter on advice to New Englanders, from Christopher Hill, *God's Englishman*.

Index